Oceanic Dance

Photographs by Franklin Marshall
Stock Photos
Ocean Line Art Illustrations by Maricela Marshall

Introduction

I grew up in the small town of Jackson, Tennessee, living on a farm far from any major waterways. The closest thing we had to water was a modest stream that ran through town, and a pond where the pigs liked to take their mud baths. That was the extent of my connection to water back then. However, in 1979, everything changed when I moved to California and found myself near the ocean for the first time. The experience was nothing short of heavenly.

A few years later, I returned to school at Cal State Monterey Bay, where I was required to take an oceanography class. Learning about the ocean was incredibly fascinating—it opened up an entirely new world to me. Our professor announced there were opportunities to intern at the Monterey National Marine Sanctuary, and though I didn't know what to expect, little did I know this would be a life-changing experience.

As an intern at the sanctuary, they asked about my skills, and I mentioned my background in running a small newspaper and knowing a bit about marketing. They were thrilled! The sanctuary was looking for ways to promote its mission, as many people were unaware of the work being done there. I came up with the idea of partnering with businesses along the coast, encouraging them to name products or services after aspects of the ocean, thereby raising awareness of the sanctuary's existence.

After graduating, I began working on a children's educational platform, using a cartoon character I had been developing for a museum project. The platform featured games and animations to teach children about ocean conservation—a cause that had become dear to me. My journey with poetry began much earlier, in seventh grade I entered a poetry contest, made it to the state level, and won! However, my friends, being musicians like me, started calling me "Shakespeare," and in those days, it wasn't a compliment. That nickname stuck, and it bothered me enough that I didn't write another poem for years.

But after my time at Cal State Monterey Bay and my experiences at the sanctuary, I felt inspired to write again—this time about the ocean. I ended up writing several poems, deeply influenced by what I had learned about the sea. Those poems sat on a shelf for a few years, until one day my wife suggested that I finish the collection. At first, I was reluctant. I was going through a period of recovery at the time and staying home, but I eventually took her advice. As I worked on completing my book of poems, new ideas began to form. I thought back to my time at the sanctuary and the educational game I had started, and it all came together. This led to the creation of an organization called Businesses for Oceanic Conservation, which encourages companies worldwide to help preserve and protect our oceans.

Now, as I look at the bigger picture—this book of 101 oceanic poems, promoting the USA's 16 National Marine Sanctuaries, expanding our children's educational games, planning a major event called the Oceanic Conference, and producing documentaries about coastal communities—I can't help but think that this is all part of a bigger plan. My wife's encouragement sparked something within me, and I believe this entire journey is a gift from God.

Contents

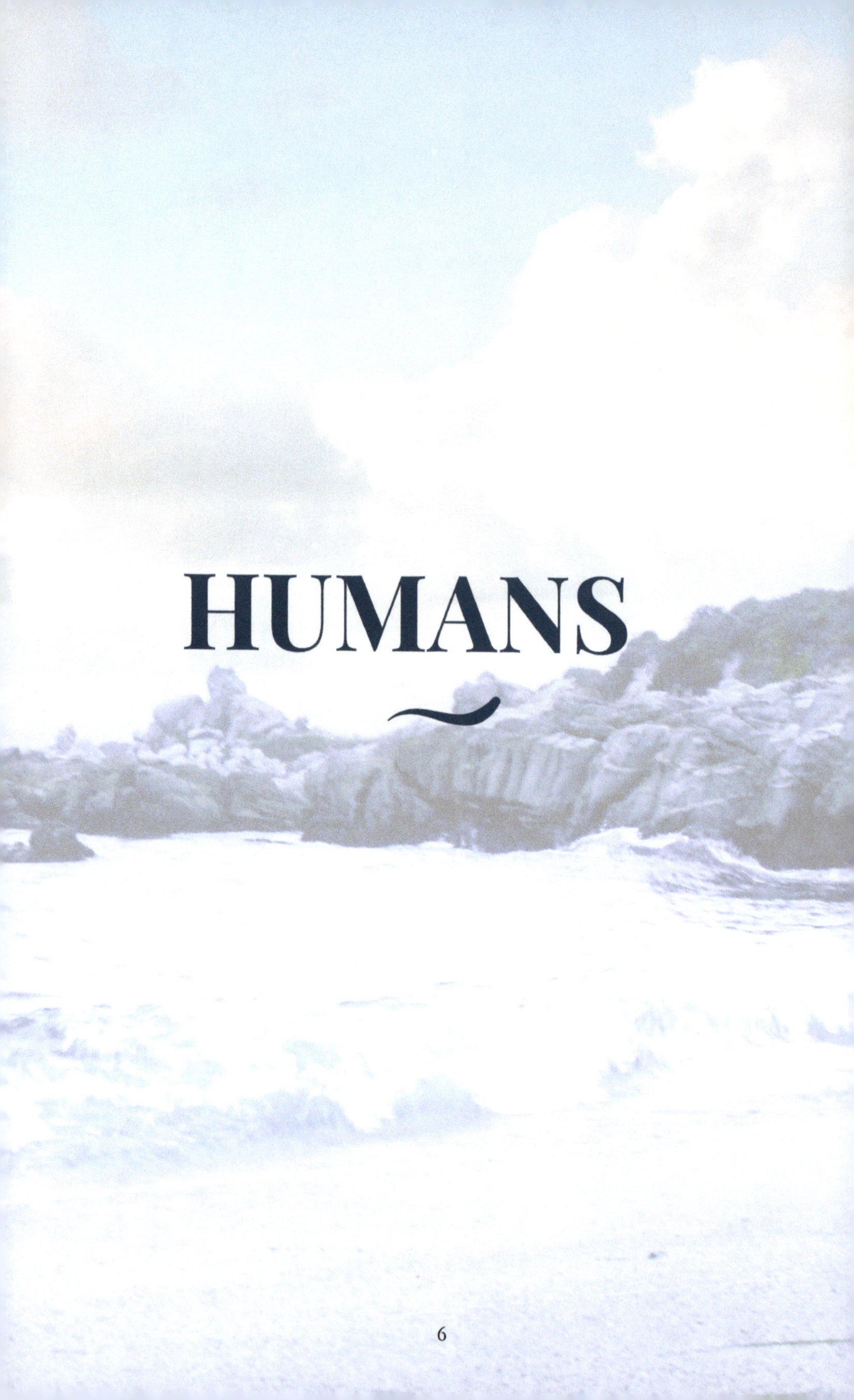

HUMANS

OCEANIC DANCE PRELUDE

I walked beside you my shadow under you holding

Your hand kicking seashells holding hands in the sand

As I clutch your arm next

To my heart, as we stopped

Going towards the sea, waves and rocks

A sunset is at hand

Afterward you sat on a rock

And kissed my palm

Then my wrist I thought

What does this mean.

Although It could mean anything; well it's

O.K. For me to interpret this gesture

As we stood embracing each other

I could feel my heart swell to

Triple time the beat and soon

I receive a kiss on the cheek

While my emotions seem to spread

Over the whole sea like a giant octopus

Loving, griping, embracing the entire body of water

With my tentacles touching every

Ocean creature with endless love

A War in the Rivers

A war was in the rivers
Marching to the sea Pesticides
and toxins Destruction far
and deep Let's make a change
To set our planet free
Clean up our oceans
Life to birds, fish and trees
We have the power
Just make a choice
To protect our environment
Let's all have a heart voice Let
us change
We have the power

Life to birds, fish and trees

Earth Wind Sky and Sea

We stand still solid on ground We
lean over in the breeze
We breathe the fresh air as we
look up
We lay in the sand watching the
waves
The earth, wind, sky and sea They
speak They sway They sob They
smile The earth, wind, sky and sea
Earth is a place to be
Wind you come so free
Sky you hold the sun
Sea where ocean life runs
The earth, wind, sky and sea

Everybody

Everybody Oceans Apart

And rivers together

We can make it moving as one

Taking care of the planet

See the ocean speak loud and clear

A million voices declaring

Save the future children can learn

Ocean life will preserve it

Everybody is one

Everybody is one with the ocean

We've got the power to

Let the whole world know

Bring all hearts as one

To let our goodness show

Surf Rider

Catch that wave
Riding the tube
Rad, radical
Surf rider

She's Everything Beautiful

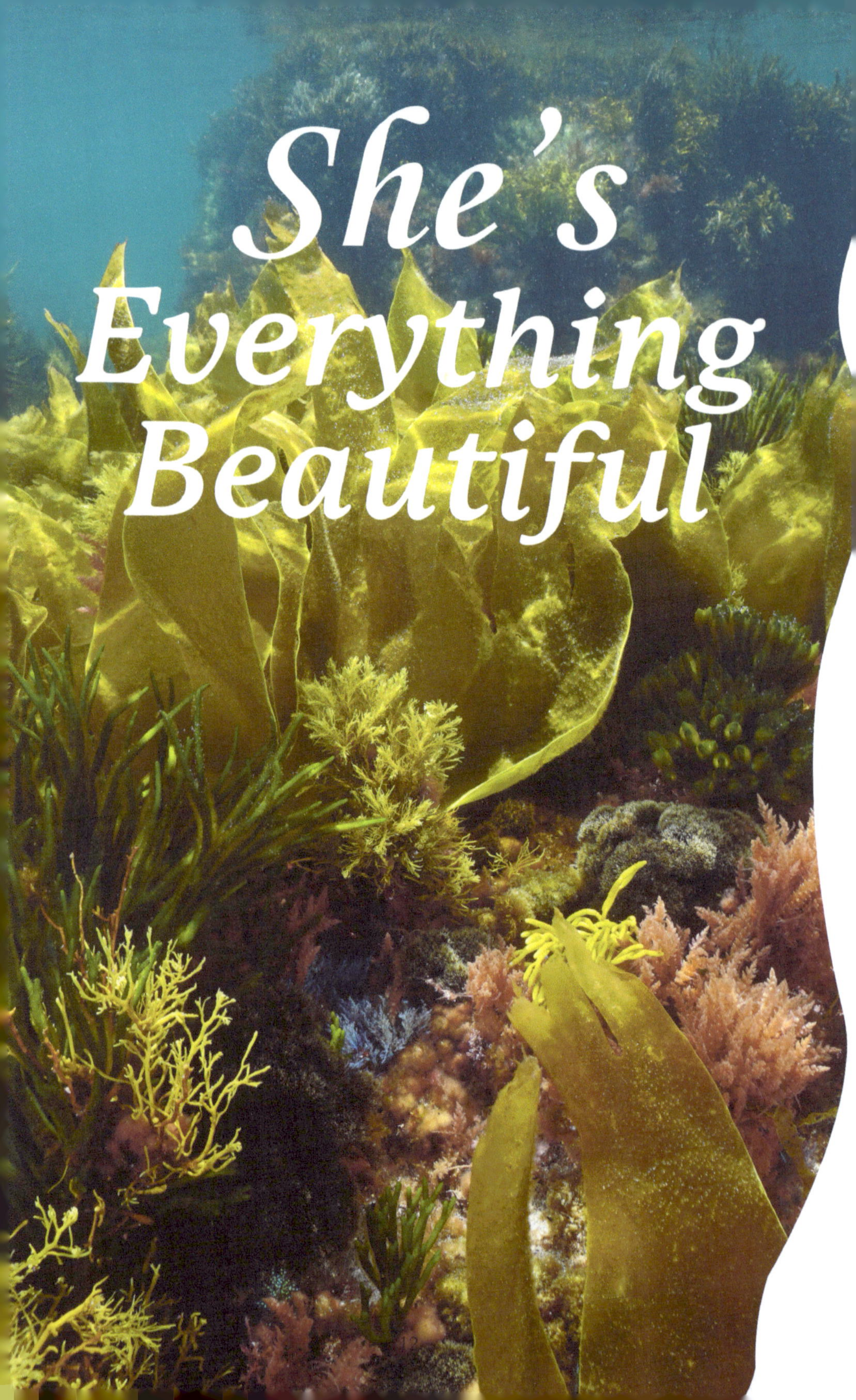

She's everything beautiful

The earth and sea the skies above

Inviting us to share our love

Protecting all as we care for her

We are the ones the chosen ones

The universe cries out to you

Heal the land please God we stand

Please heal our land

Polluted ocean's scream how will they learn?

When will they know?

My aches and pains they're washed ashore

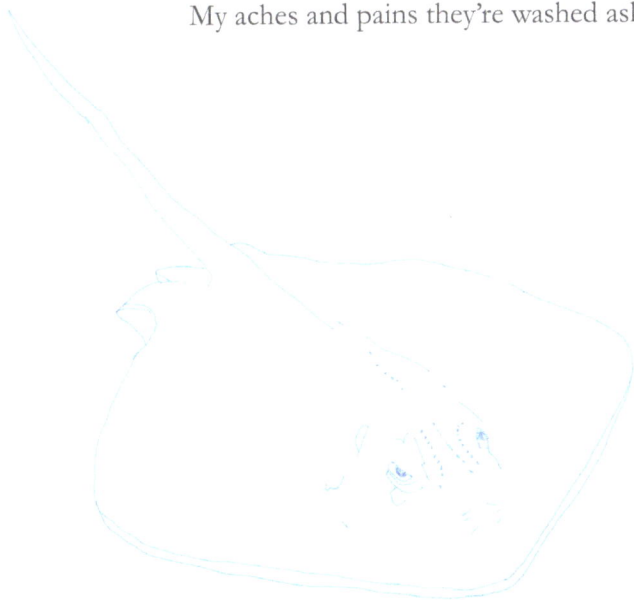

Save Our
SHORES

For the little ones
For the older ones
For our humanity
Save our shores

Cruise Blues

A sunny day

With cheerful thoughts
I see the sky

I sail the sea
Living loving them both
Cruise Blues

Light House is
Home

Darkness storms and rain

Crashing waves seemed insane

Off course a cry afar

Direct my course onto shore

Lighthouse to come

Lighthouse is home

Lighthouse I long

As day at sea is done.

A Place of Turbulent
Rest

I bow my head
Arms gently tucked in my lap
Peace I hear, comfort I breathe A
place of turbulent rest. Energy
from the Sea
Rich Bright Thrust
You are igniting
That revolution a new
Must see a new day

Energy from the sea.

Smile

In The Sand

I like to see your smile

Hearing the gentle sound of your voice

In the sea I love to lie in the sand

Capturing the essence of all

The rays of your love

You make me feel enthroned

The waves as they crash are like

Heaven looking down upon me

You are lovely

You are joy

Pray For The
SEA

All heads are bowed
As we pray for the sea.
We beg the heavens
For all darkness to flee
Its boundless grace, its depth, its might,
For protection and grace, we seek the light.
The waves that carry hopes and fears,
The tides that wash away the tears.
We pray for the sea, its endless blue,
For in its vastness, we pray
The troubles are few.
So let us cherish, guard, and keep, the
Ocean's song, both wild and deep.
With every prayer, let our love be,
A promise made, as we pray for the sea.

Oceanic

DANCE

Story

You stroked my hair with your hand

And it seemed to be filled with length And growth of a foot long upon each touch I won't soon forget the aroma Of your sent mingled with the Ocean mist a gentle breeze and the warm sand Oh how do I capture this moment to Embrace it for eternity As my tentacles release the grip Of your irresistible embrace I could see afar off as it Came so near the waves Crashing so calm and a reflection Of my heart in cove grove Doing the oceanic dance For a moment and then a while The looming quest to know What, how, where? Is it real? What if it is just a dream? Although dreams do come true I reach for you once more To confirm this moment of ecstasy As we walked back along the trail

Hearing the waves still in that Majestic
moment these impressions That I
experienced gripping and embracing
Thoughts of the sea and the oceanic
dance Filled my emotions The memory
of this moment will Be etched upon the
tables of my heart And soul as the artist
carves a stone Please memory never
forget those Days of romantic beginnings
Never leave me always come back Return
forever Even when I rock in my Chair
And remember a moment of the past As
we approach the street Where our cars
are parked My longing dream is only to
Relive this romance a Thousand times
over When I reach for the handle Of the
car door it seems to remind Me of the
grip of holding Hands on the beach I
slowly get in my car starting It and
driving, gazing, reminded Of the place
and moment on the beach Where the
oceanic dance was so clear In my
thoughts all I could do now is to long To
relive this delight Fighting, viciously to
recall Every minute, second we touched
My cell phone rings, I can only hope That
my love will I yet again have more
Real state of romance to accentuate the thrill

Of a longing for love

Yes it is my sweetheart calling Oh how I want the call never to End my insatiable obsession For my Love will never end Now the phone call has ended only to Embark upon a fresh thrill that Won't release my invited desire This blossom that arrays itself upon my intimate longing extracts a teardrop mixed ambitions that I can only express to my love Even a teardrop falls from my cheek Oh no why am I crying or is It really crying for what I thought As the water poured from my cheek With a smile on my face the ocean of tears Become the place and moment of The oceanic dance and even now That through my tears I can see so Clear. My love I thought is Here with me forever After a while and I've made It home longing to drift away Into the memory of the day And yes the beach my love and the Oceanic dance The quest for the moment to remember is so strong I thirst For that time to come back to me. I look for something to sooth my thirst, a cup, a glass the first thing I could find was cold water in the sea I smiled as I gripped the glass

I gently set the glass on the table and
Leaned back and look upon the Cold glass of
Water I thought Is this true or just in my head
Upon This water the dance appears
The oceanic dance seems so real
I think it is. I reach to touch
The dance as I reach for the glass
It slips to spill the water
On the tables glass top
As I leap to save the glass the spill
The water consumes the entire table
I looked for a towel a napkin anything
To stop the water spread
The groove is on with the oceanic
Dance I thought it would stop but
it only grew, beating, growing, moving
pulsating to a tune of love reliving
the moment with my love on the beach
What is it about the water
The tears the glass of water
And ocean that brings the oceanic dance
It's like a thought to relive the
Looming long love fest that I can
Never forget
When the night falls and I prepare to rest my
Head upon my pillow no other day has been
In my life so full of love thoughts
Rest a sweet dream appears I open
My heart to its lure
As I prepare to dream I'm given
A chose I choose the oceanic
Dance rest is sweet I rest Dream
flowing brooks streams of passion

Leading to that ocean of love
Like the octopus tentacles
caving The entire sea Awake,
awake my internal Alarm calls
me back to a bright Sun Shine a
lovely day. Longing for a
soothing shower To wake me
for the day The water drip
drops till the spray Overwhelms
the wall behind me And I can't
believe my eyes My heart swells
my thoughts Rush am I still
dreaming The water on the wall
of the Shower there appears a
reminder Of the time and space
at the Beach with my love the
Water seems to hold the
memory Of the oceanic dance
the Longing desire to be
together I can't explain Longing
to relive the beach The touch
the smell of my love The
oceanic dance A phone call I
have no chose But the desire
overwhelms me Every thought
how I long to walk On the
beach holding hands We talk on
the phone the voice Of my
desire awaits me yes We will
relive the oceanic dance The
rush to see your face to feel
Your embrace permeates every
Crevice of my being

How to keep you clean

I wash you up

And blow you down

But still standing is a mountain

The vastness of humans

Unwanted treasures

How can I keep you clean

They soap you down with showers

Of millions and thousands

Unrelenting mass descending

Amount of food for thought

But I know it's not the heath we sought

How to keep you clean

We see we smile at your splendor

No gender encompassing it all on both sides

We think we know the beauty you show

Ocean how to keep you clean

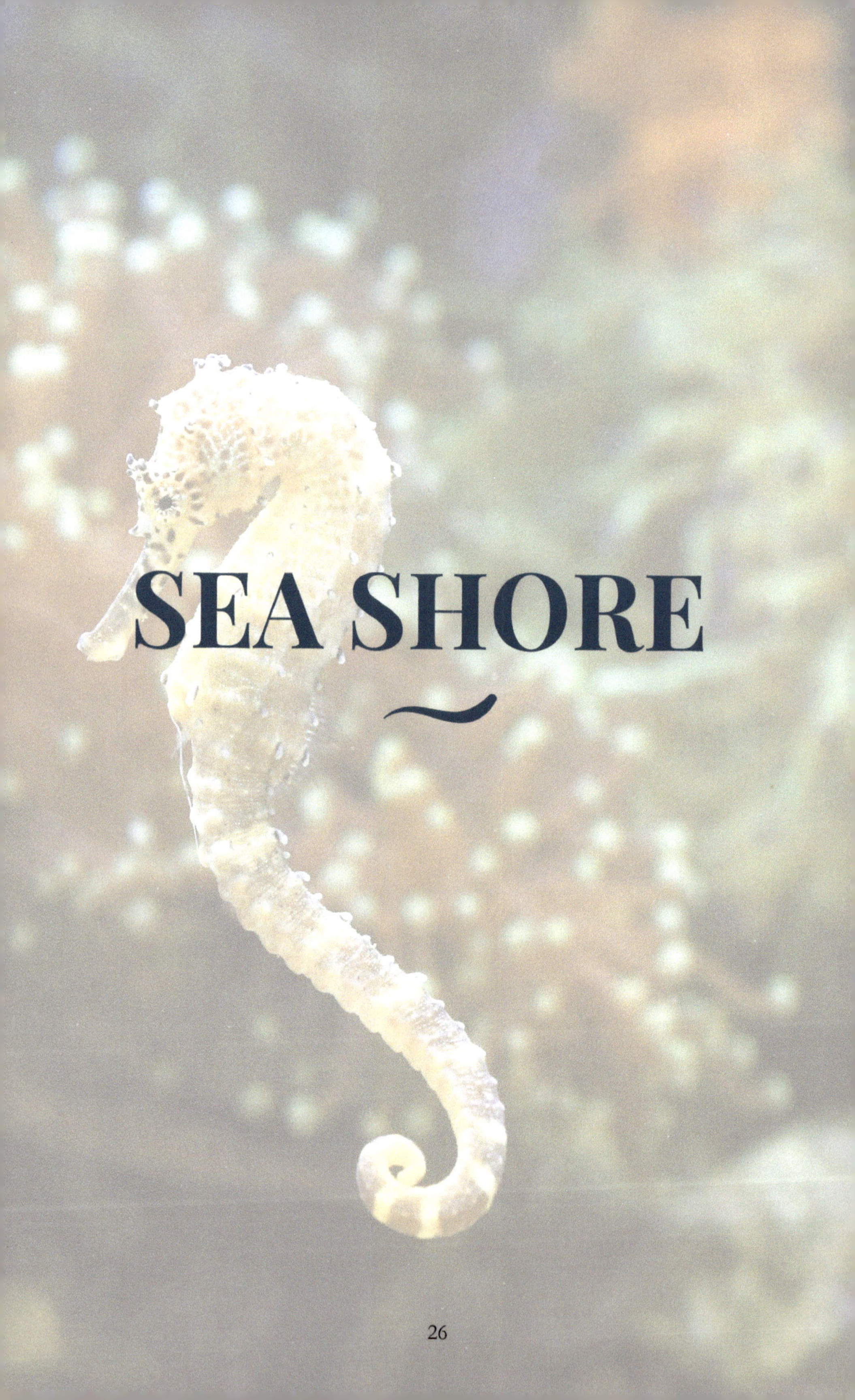

SEA SHORE

We Move To The Beat

. We Move To The Beat
We move to the beat
The rhythm of the waves
Pulsating water crash ashore
Soaring are swells of joy
Oceanic dance is on

Oceanic dance is fun

Crying Ocean

I feel your pain
I see your cry
Crying ocean I see you die
We've come to help
To save your day
When ocean life can return to stay
To joyful times Oh how we wait
Please come back To the years before
When life was blissful
From times gone past

Ocean Parade

They danced with hands

The songs reach far

Ocean parade Ocean parade

That's what you are

An array of colors

A party is on The mating song is heard

A whale of a good time will come

Sea life parade

From coast to coast

A world of vibrant life

Diving and ocean tourists Like it the most

Ocean parade Blue, Turquoise many colors displayed

Ocean parade

We all celebrate your masquerade

Traveling Waves

Floating on salt

I can live on you

Brown pelican drink

California

Coastal sea brew

Rainy sea

A veil of mist, the rainy sea,

Where droplets fall and set free
A canvas grey, a muted light,
In rain's embrace, the sea's delight.
The waves, they whisper soft and low,
Beneath the rain's persistent flow.
Rainy sea, a world subdued,
In every drop, the mood's renewed.
A gentle touch, a soothing sound,
Where sea and sky are tightly bound.
Rainy sea, in its quiet might,
Holds the day and cradles night

Ocean Moon

A silver disc, adrift and alone,
No light in sight, it casts its own.
The ocean moon, on high it beams,
A dreamy glow, on rippling streams.
The waves below, in silent chase,
Reflect the moon, a mirrored grace.
An enchanting ballet, a lunar spell,
Where secrets sleep, and stories
dwell.
The ocean whispers, soft and low,
As tides rise and mysteries flow.
Beneath the moon, a world to
explore,
The ocean lives, and we stand in
awe.

Green is Blue

I knew you green
You gleam debris
The vain connecting every stream
Traveling to blue oceans
Green is blue
Green is the foundation
To the movement
That brought us blue
Green is life
Green is blue
The ocean the sky
Even how we think

Sandy
SHORES

Blooms magnificently adorned

Here rock cluster form

Mounted shapes hold the sand

Granite mountain Now at hand

Sandy shores they were

Sandy shores now rocks and sand

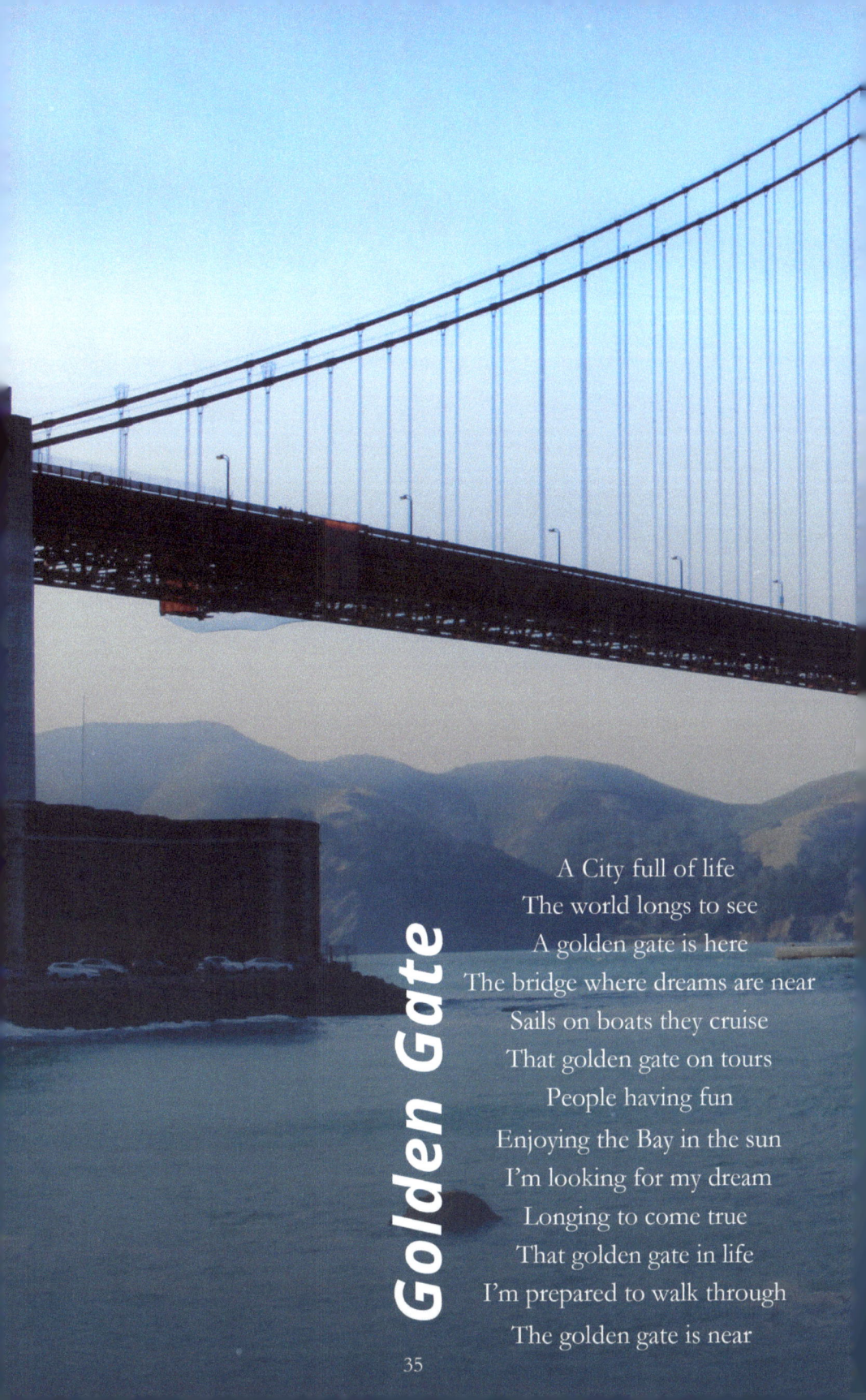

Golden Gate

A City full of life
The world longs to see
A golden gate is here
The bridge where dreams are near
Sails on boats they cruise
That golden gate on tours
People having fun
Enjoying the Bay in the sun
I'm looking for my dream
Longing to come true
That golden gate in life
I'm prepared to walk through
The golden gate is near

Golden
Anchor

Golden Anchor I am
They call me deep
My grip is to hold and keep
Secure stable in place
Heaped is the water stacked and
pressed upon me
As I willing take a rest
I reach for the ocean floor
Yes my umbilical cord reaches from
the ship to the bottom of the sea
I am and willing shall be forever that
Golden Anchor to hold you steady in
a place to keep

Breakers

As breakers rise in their foamy crest,

They're something straight out of a treasure chest

Like majestic sheets moving to and fro
Across the ocean, in waves they go
They travel far, with winds they play,
Across the blue, they make their way,
Their strength upon the shore they fling,
A symphony of waves they sing.
In their retreat, they leave behind,
A trace of sea foam, soft and kind.
Their gentle touch upon the land,
The touch of nature's artful hand.

Breeze
Relief

Beneath the stars, the ocean is still,

No stirring waves, or a windy ordeal

The air hangs heavy, thick and hot,

A stifling breath, a sailors' knot.

But from the east, a whisper starts,

A ripple forms and tugs at hearts.

The ocean stirs, a gentle sigh,

As cooling winds begin to fly.

Across the waves, the currents race,

With playful dance and a cool embrace.

The salty spray the ocean's kiss,

Replaces heat with a peaceful bliss

Ocean At My
Door

The ocean's breath upon my
door,
Its salty kiss, a siren's
lore.
With every tide that comes and goes,
A story of the deep it shows.
The waves, they whisper tales of
yore,
Of sailors' dreams and legends'
core.
The ocean at my door does beat,
In this embrace of sea and
shore,
I find a peace not felt before.
The ocean's vast, my door ajar,

Together, they erase each scar.

Hot

SEA

Beneath the
scorching sun's fierce glow,
The hot sea whispers, as it
dances to and fro.

Its waves like molten glass in the sun they shine,

In every crest, nature's wondrous unique design.

The steam ascends to meet the day,

As waters dance in as if in a Shakespearean play.

The hot sea's breath, a sultry veil,

Where sun and ocean's powers prevail.

In this warm embrace of tide and light,

The sea aflame with day's bright might.

A hot sea's song, both bold and free,

In every wave, life's fiery spree.

Ocean
VIEW

With eyes cast out to endless blue,

The ocean view, forever true.

Like DaVinci's canvas, a painter's dream.

In every shade of blue

nature's creme de la creme.

The horizon whispers to the soul,

Of journeys far and tales untold.

The ocean view, a constant muse,

In its depths, the world's hues fuse.

A gaze that holds both storm and calm.

The sea's embrace, a healing balm.

The ocean view, from dawn till night,

A vision of the world's pure light

Sea Vision

Through the lens of sea vision so clear,
The world's edge seems to draw near.
A vast stretch, expanding, where
dreams take flight,
In the sea's depths, there's no night.
The colors blend, from green to blue,
A sea vision of every hue.
Where dolphins leap and corals bloom,
Life's tapestry in ocean's room.
With sea vision, we see the truth,
Of nature's fountain, its eternal youth.
The sea, a guide, a timeless mission,
In every wave, a clear vision.

Trouble Waters

Chaos beneath the surface lies
Symbolic of the storms that
arise. In troubled waters,
I search for peace A
calm within the depths,
a world to cease. The
waves crash as the
currents sway
As I try to make
my way away from
the darkest bay.
Darkness lurks
beneath, like the
devil's nest. Fear
grips my wrists like
the troubled demons
at rest. But even in
turmoil, I'll find a
way to ride the waves
and to face the day.
For in the depth of the
sea and the deep deep
blue lies a hidden strength,
waiting to break through.

Wave Blast

A sudden surge, a wall of
white, the waves explode
with frightening might.
The ocean's fist, a
crushing blow, on sandy
shores, the torrents flow.
The wind whips fierce,
the air it stings, as
seagulls cry on broken
wings. It lifts debris,
from sea and sand,
a fleeting storm
of nature's hand.
The foamy crest,
a moment's reign,
recedes softly, to
charge again. But on
the shore, no marks
remain. A wave blast
echoes, but leaves
no stain.

Washed Away

The tide surges in relentless sweeps,
Clawing at shores, the ocean creeps.
Sandcastles crumble, dreams washed away,
Ephemeral sculptures of yesterday.
Luminous under moon's soft glow,
They dance where tides ebb and flow.
With caps like gossamer, they show,
The art of living soft and slow.
In currents' grasp, they sway and shift,
No anchor, no burden, just a gift.
The sea's own stars, they lift,
The jellyfish, nature's silent drift.

Lost At Sea

Adrift at sea, a single speck,
I tap my compass, it's broken neck.
No guiding star, no welcoming shore,
Just endless waves and a chilling roar.
In squawks and calls, their tales are spun,
Of fish below, and radiant sun.
With feathers white, like foam on sea,
They claim the breeze, wild and free.
At day's end, as the sun dips low,
They perch on sands, in twilight's glow.
Their day's work done, in silence, they huddle,
Dreaming of skies, where they merrily pubble.

Ocean
LOVE

The ocean's heart is wide and true,
In crashing waves, and depths of blue.
It calls on me with siren's song,
To watery depths where I belong.
Tides beckon and winds entrance, in
soft white ripples, my fingers dance.
Beneath the clouds, a whispered vow,
to love the ocean, here and now.
Its mysteries are a sacred treasure, to
search for them is my greatest pleasure.
With every tide, my love grows deeper,
to be bound in the ocean's arms
forever.

Morning
Breeze

The first blush creeps, a rosy hue, A gentle wind makes all things new.

Across the waves, it lightly skims,
Chasing away the night's cold whims.
A new day on the endless coast,

The sun rises beyond the salty host.

The sleeping sails begin to rise,
As masts reach high towards the skies.
Seabirds call, a joyful sound,
As sunlight paints the ocean's ground.
The morning air, a sweet release,
Ushers in new joy and peace

Misty Ocean

A shroud of grey, the misty ocean,
A world in soft, perpetual motion.
The fog caresses each gentle wave,
In its quiet realm, the sea's enclave.
The misty ocean, a dreamer's land,
Where water meets the sky's soft hand.
A canvas blurred, where seagulls soar, Above the
whispers of the shore.
In this hazy veil, the world's unseen,
A tranquil, misty ocean's sheen.
A place of peace, where thoughts can roam,
In the ocean's mist, we find our home.

Silhouette Sea

Against the dusk, the silhouette sea,

Contours sharp in the fading lee.

dance of shadows upon the tide,

In the evening's arms, the
waves confide.

The silhouette sea, a
darkened grace,

A moving painting, no

artist's trace. Its form

outlined by the last day's

light, a fleeting

beauty, soon lost to night.

In this realm of contrast,
stark and sheer

he silhouette sea draws us near.

A moment's glimpse into the deep,

Before the night's embrace, in silence steep.

Majestic Waves

Majestic and strong as they fall and
rise,
The waves of nature, a power with no
disguise.
Their crests like crowns of frothy lace,
Upon the sea, they claim their space.
With thunderous roar, they crash and
churn,
In their might, the oceans twist and
turn.
Majestic waves, with each attack and
retreat,
Leave tales of old at the shore's sandy
feet.
A dance of chaos and of grace,
In every wave, the sea's
embrace.
Majestic waves, in endless flow,
In their strength, the winds do blow.

Stormy Shores

Upon the stormy shores, the tempest roars,
A symphony, symbolic of winds and wars.
The waves lash out with furious might,
Against the shore, in endless fight.
The skies alight with lightning's fire,
A canvas vast of nature's ire.
Stormy shores, where seagulls cry,
Beneath the brooding, angry sky.
Yet in this chaos, beauty thrives,
As every wave, the shore revives.
Stormy shores, in power's hold,
A story of resilience, ageold.

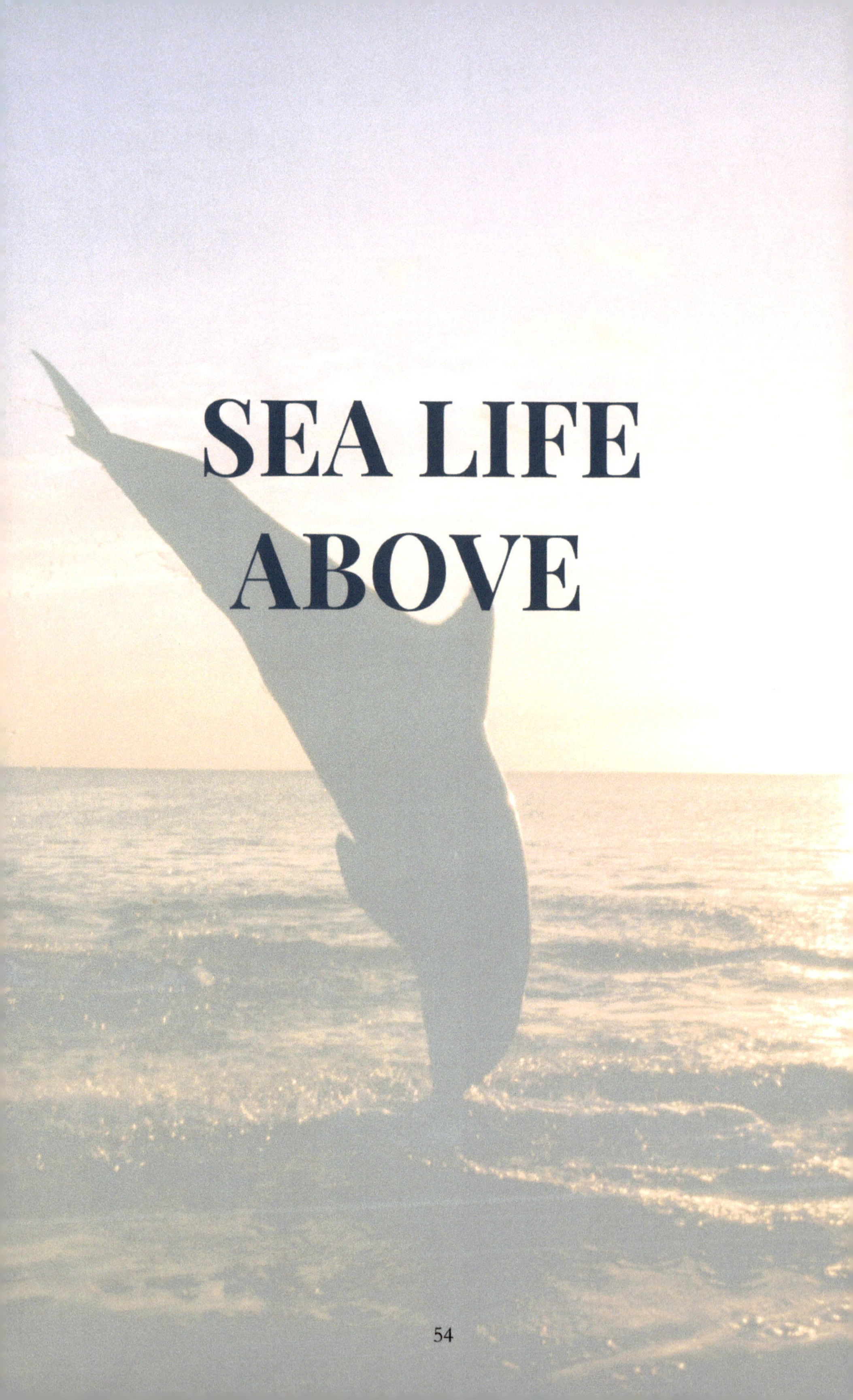

SEA LIFE ABOVE

Sails of Joy

Sails soar sensationally far

Breezes beckon the morning sun

Melting tight fog exposing

Sails of joy are soon to come

Salt Water Breeze

You breath and flatter with mist

Reaching from far and wide

Your grip is so divine

Thrilled arrayed so kind

Wasting no time with

Your tender embrace

Saltwater breeze

Come spray your unrelenting

Showers of smiles upon my face

Saltwater breeze

You reach you rise to

The top

Acceleration, ascension

Dimension, attention

We long for

Saltwater breeze

Saltwater breeze you are

California Condor

You soar high

Gazing beneath Please tell me
What do you see
Let me know what to do

I long to help California condor

Sea Birds

Sea Bird I saw
Float flight ashore
Displayed elegance
Your longevity is core

Garden of God

Garden of God Majesty
Wind, water, nature and everything
Beautiful oh sunshine
Let it blow let it flow let it sing
Deep within we all know
God planet universe we are one
Protect the land, sky and sea
We'll live in peace in harmony
Garden of God yes we can
Take care protect this beautiful land
For all life every living thing
God, planet, universe, yes we can

Ocean Birds fly

Ocean Birds fly
Whales sing a song
Coral reef sway
As sea life roam
A pleasure we love
Ocean beaches for us
Our ocean deep friends
Need help again and again
We are their voices
Spreading messages
Far and near
God save this planet
Just help us all to hear.

WHITE SNOWY PLOVER

White snowy Plover

Delight graceful in the sand

Young chicks thrive if they can

Make way for birds and beach

This is Snowy Plover's land to keep

Ocean In The Sky

The world inverts, an artist's muse,
A mirrored world, in sapphire hues.
Pelicans soar, in a feathered ballet,
Dipping their beaks, in the clouds of the
day.
The ocean in the sky, a whimsical
sight,
White birds dancing, in the
ethereal light. Is it water they
seek, or a wispy white prize?
Perhaps stolen starlight, for

their hungry eyes.
Below, the true sea, crashes on
the shore,
But these feathered hunters, forever
explore.
A reminder that wonders, can take many
forms,
Where the sky meets the ocean, in magical storms.

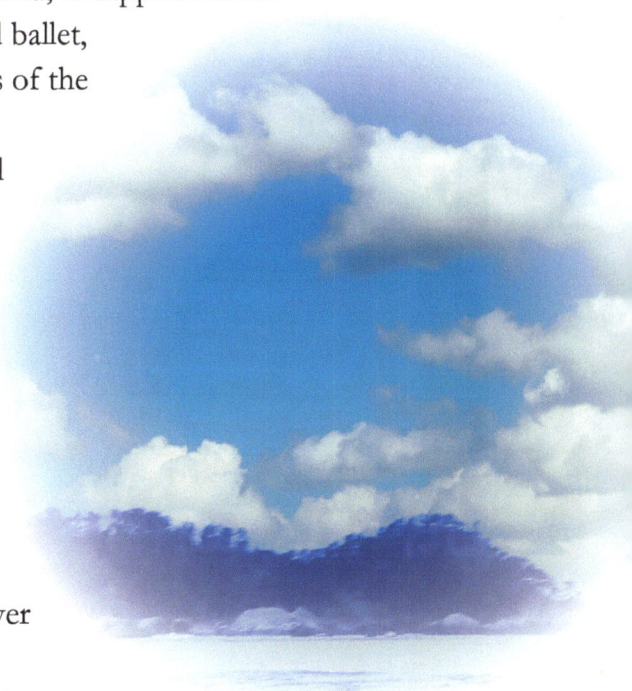

SEA LIFE

Leather Back

Leather back, back down
To Baja, Costa Rica, California
And beyond
Leather Back fly high leap low
Glide, ride the waves
From shore to shore
You know how this game is played
No paper back, leather back

OCTOPUS

Embraced wrapped

Intertwined

You reach deep and far

Long and wide

Octopus you are

Like a thousand triangles

Connected as one

As two become lovers

With your extensive reach

Octopus you are so deep

Salmon Said

River by river
Streams my path
Day by night a search a destiny
The pass their future
Their hunger fulfilled
Spare life streams yield
Ocean clean human see
Make way give chance

For young life salmon said
Give me a chance to come
Back from the insatiable
Appetite of my diminished
Ocean friends acknowledge when
I haven't said too much but
They saw me running up the streams
Down the creeks
They thought I was finished
Salmon said

Salmon said

Jelly
Fish

Jellyfish

Jellyfish Your electrified kiss

I see you through

Your magnification ablest

Sea
Paradise

Like no other
Gazing beneath
Radiant brilliant sea life

Sea paradise

Otter Smile

Immeasurable rewards hope to gain

Restful sea otter smile
Otter smile
Because you rest secure
With peaceful thoughts that's for sure.

Squid Row

We gather
We line up

Unified we float
Casting our connectors
Coasting through the sea

We move we glide
Down and up

Squid Row

Rock On The
Shore

A weathered rock, on sandy shore,
Has stood for ages and seen so much more.

A silent witness, strong and grand,
To ships that sail and shifting sand.
A starfish stranded, a crimson display,
Five reaching arms grasp at the day.
Left by the tide, a fleeting guest,
Yearning for depths, where it may rest.
The rock, unmoving, a silent friend,
Offers respite, till the ocean ascends.
Together they watch, the endless chase,
Of sun and moon, in an infinite embrace.

Oceans Everywhere

In raindrops soft that kiss the ground,
As the waters in oceans all around.
Not only shores where the waters crash high,
But pulsing waves beneath the summer sky.
A lobster scuttles, with claws so strong,
Across the seabed, where it belongs.
Every creature, great and small,
The ocean's arms are welcoming to all.
From mountain peak to desert's heart,
The ocean's touch is a hidden art.
For life itself, from sea it rose,
The water's song in all that flows.

The
Valley Of
The Sea

In the deep blue sea, where shadows hide,

A realm of wonder where secrets reside.

The currents cradle, a hush descends,

Stories untold, where adventure transcends.

In this valley of wonder far from the shore,

A sea horse gallops along the ocean floor.

Guided by the current, it moves with grace,

Swayed by the gentle touch of this sacred place.

The sea's soft whisper, like a kiss to the ear,

Through the valley it wipes away all the fear.

Like a mysterious avenue, an ocean's alley,

Is the beauty of the sea, deep in that valley

Bless The Water

Bless the water, life's sweet art,

With hand upraised and a grateful heart,
From crystal clouds, it gently falls,
A gift that quenches, heals, and calls.
Bless the dolphins, with playful leaps,
Arching through waves, where sunlight peeps.
Their whistles echo, a joyous sound,
Guardians of magic, forever unbound.

Bless the currents, that softly sway,
Carrying life on their endless way.
So, thank the water, pure and bright,

A source of life, a sacred light.

Free Water

A gift from skies, to earth it flows,
In rivers wide, the free water goes.
It quenches thirst, it gives us life,
In its journey, ends all strife.
Black seals bask on rocks, sleek and free,
Onyx eyes gleaming in sunlit glee.
They plunge and frolic in childish delight,
A symphony of life, in this cool respite.
It binds us all, a common thread,
From sky to sea, its path is led.
Let us cherish the flow, the endless song,
Free water's magic, where we all belong.

Sand To Sea

Through broken shells, small heads
break free,
A hoard of baby turtles begin their
journey.
One by one, hatchlings join the
spree,
A blanket of shells, crawling to the
sea.
Flippers dig deep, with a determined
beat,
Pushing through sand, a challenging
feat.
Each step they take, away from sandy
grave,
Waiting for the grip of a friendly
wave.
From sand to sea, a dance of fate,
A race for the tide, no time to
waste.
Then finally, the voyage is complete,

When salty water and new borns
meet.

Blue Waters

In the realm where blue waters
run,
The sky and the sea become
one.
A canvas for the sun's beaming
rays,
A reflection of an ethereal
daze.
A humpback whale breaches, a majestic
sight,
A leviathan rising, bathed in
sunlight.
Barnacled back gleams, a fleeting
show,
As it arches its form in a graceful
flow.
Then a haunting song, a mournful
cry,
Echoes through waves, reaching to the
sky.
A symphony deep, of rhythm and
blues,
The sounds of the ocean and breathtaking
views.

Sunset At Sea

The sky is painted red and gold,

As sunset falls, the sea grows old.

Seabirds and otters come out to play,

As day gives way to endless bay.

In the kelp where the sea otters play,

They twirl and they spin in a watery ballet.

With fur so dense, it keeps them afloat,

As they lie on their backs, like a furry boat.

As the sun sets, they rest in the kelp's gentle hold,

Their whiskered faces, expressions bold.

In the sea's lullaby, they drift to sleep,

The sea otters' dreams, in the deep, so sweet.

Sea Smile

The sea smile spreads a radiant glow
From east to west, from high to low
As it dances on the waters, shone so bright
A soft touch, like rays of sunlight
But beneath the surface, a glint of
steel,
A flash of teeth, a hunger
revealed.
The shark, a hunter, a
primal force, A hidden
smile, on a silent course.

In the sea's smile, I find my
peace
A sense of calm and warmth, like
fleece
With depth I can see the ocean's grace
A smile that echoes a warm embrace

Sands Of
Time

The ocean drums a timeless beat,

As the grains of time begin to meet.

A shoreline vast, a simple rhyme,

Where the past rests, in sands of time.

Beneath the tide, where waters hum,

The clams reside, in silence, numb.

In sandy beds, they rest and wait,

The ocean's calm, their steady state.

No lofty flight, no soaring high,

Yet in their depths, true treasures lie.

In stillness, clams their stories weave,

Of ocean's gifts, which they receive.

Night
Wave

Beneath the moon's soft silvery gaze,

Long after the daytime chaos and haze
The sea whispers secrets, old and grave,
In the gentle rocking of the night wave.
He dives with a twist, through the emerald brine,
Amongst the fish that dart and the sea stars that shine.
His bark echoes deep, through the saltsprayed air,
A call of the wild, free from any care.
As dusk paints the sky with a palette so wide,

The sea lion returns with the turn of the tide.
On the rock, he will rest, 'neath the moon's silver crown
The king of the coast, in his fur robe of brown.

Flat Sea

Acalm expanse, the flat sea lies,
Beneath the dome of sprawling
skies. No ripple stirs its glassy face,
In stillness, still, it finds its grace.
A master of disguise, in the
ocean's hold, Camouflaged
against the seabed's gold.
It waits in patience,
for a meal to stray,
A silent hunter, in the
blue's ballet. With a
flick of fin, it's gone
from sight, A ghostly
shadow, in the water's
light. The halibut's
journey, a silent tale,
In the ocean's chorus,
it sets sail.

Restless Waters

Restless waters,never still,
A world in motion, like
clockwork, a drill.
The waves they toss,
the currents race,
In their turmoil,
a wild embrace.
In the silence
of the
underwater
realm,
The oyster
reigns, a
stoic helm.
With layers of
nacre, it toils away,
Crafting beauty,
day by day.
A treasure chest in
a sea so vast,
The oyster's gift,
meant to last.
In its quiet labor,
a gem does bloom,
A secret wonder,
in the ocean's womb.

Raining Waves

Upon the sea, the raindrops weave,
A tapestry of raining waves they heave
As each droplet stirs a tiny, little crest,
In the ocean's vast, unending quest.
With faces friendly, whiskers that feel,
They graze on greens, their favorite meal.
In groups they gather, in peace they reel,
The sea cows' charm, it's quite real.
At day's close, when light fades to dreams,
Manatees rest in moonlit streams.
In the quiet lull, the water gleams,
As they drift in sleep, in soft moonbeams.

Wet Waves Winter

In winter's grip, the wet waves churn,

Against the chill, they twist and turn.
A frosted breath upon the sea,
Where waves embrace the cold, yet free.
In the land of ice, where cold winds blow,
The penguin waddles through the snow.
Black and white, in stark contrast,
Against the ice, they're unsurpassed.
They slide on bellies, sleek and fast,
In the frozen world, vast and vast.
With flippers like wings, they cannot soar,

But in the water, they explore.

Waves
Big

Waves big,with mighty heave,

A force that makes the bravest grieve.

They rise like mountains from the deep,

In their wake, the world does weep.

In the depths where the currents flow,

The Sea bass swims, steady and slow.

A flash of silver in the deep blue sea,

Gliding through waves, wild and free.

As twilight falls, they find their rest,

In the ocean's arms, they're truly blessed.

The Seabass journey, silent and vast,

Walking On Water

Like a dance with nature, a wonder to please
On waves of blue, I step with ease
The liquid surface, pathway divine
As I walk on water, we start to intertwine
In the vast blue where silence reigns,
The humpback whale sings its refrains.
A melody deep, that travels far,
A song of the sea, from star to star.
In the deep, it roams, a gentle giant,
Through the marine world, tranquil and pliant.
The humpback's journey, through seas uncurled,
A wondrous being, in a watery world.

DEEP SEA

We Walk in the Sea

You are kelp a place of refuge
Walking tall in the sea
You hang deep beneath the shores
Kelp for all species on ocean floors
Your vast reach invites the sun
Beaming through while ocean work is done
Extending your ground by the minute hour and day
We walk in the sea kelp forest
Rooted far beneath
We walk in the sea
And float to the sand
Kelp forest an important use for many
Providing for many for endless times.

Caves of salt

I can't resist
Deep beneath
The ocean floor
Brilliantly wise
Does knowledge pour

Forest in the
Deep

You flow your low down
Dirty colorful full of mysteries exquisite
Forest in the deep
You've taken many lives
In the deep to the depth
While giving birth to new elements of life
Forest in the deep
Why do you rage so angrily
While whisper so gently

Coral Melody

Sing songs of radiant

Unbelievable melodies

Dazzling lines

Syncopated rhythms

Of fusion over tones

With angelic life joining the coral melody

Resounding from the walls

Of dustless shores

Coral Melody sings their songs

On Ocean floors

The symphony moves on

With scores of tunes until coral melody

Singsong true

Help us leave the nets behind

We'll play, dance, and sing

Then will coral melody will chime

Crystal Pearls

Your value exceeds all pearls
Worth more than diamonds
Gold and all precious jewels
Where are you from?
Who is so lucky to possess your
crystal pearl?

So Deep

Down where nighttime reigns supreme,
Creatures of the deep blue dream. Here,
squids like phantoms, glide and weave,
Ten writhing arms, the currents cleave.

Glowing tentacles, an eerie light,
Octopi dance in the endless night
Eight long limbs in fleeting shrouds,

Disappear into in the inky clouds.
Beneath the waves, in silence vast,
The ocean's heart beats slow and fast.

In this realm of quiet, dark and deep,
Creatures of the deep blue crawl to sleep.

Mountains at
SEA

Beneath the waves, a great treasure
lies
A silent strength beneath the
skies.
The mountains at sea, a sight to
behold,
Their stories of grandeur, centuries
old.
They stand as sentinels, tall and
grand,
Where waves meet rock, they proudly
stand.
A testament to Earth's
artistry,
These towering forms in the vast
sea.
In their shadows, secrets
dwell,
Of ocean's depth and stormy
swell.
Mountains at sea, their tops a
dome
In their steadfastness, we find
home.

Sea Weeds

In ocean's garden, beneath the wave,

The sea weeds dance, the sea weeds sway.
A forest green, where life abounds,

In their embrace, the sea's heart pounds.
Kelp forests rise in a tangled maze,
Sheltering creatures in a playful daze.
Tiny fish dart in a display of color,
While shrimp and crabs entertain each other.
Salmon glide by, with scales so bright,
Resting their journey, in the cool, green light.
Fed and recharged, they go on their way,
But the sea weeds await them another day.

Black
SEA

A shroud of mystery, the Black Sea lies
Under moonlit skies, its echoes rise.
A hidden world, where shadows play,
Where old shipwrecks never fade away.
On rocky crags, like a spiky shroud,
Sea urchins cling, a prickly crowd.
Spines like needles, a watchful hoard,
Against the currents they fiercely guard.
This sea of ebony, silent and limber,
Grasps the earth in its endless slumber.
The Black Sea, with its quiet might,
Guards its secrets from the light.

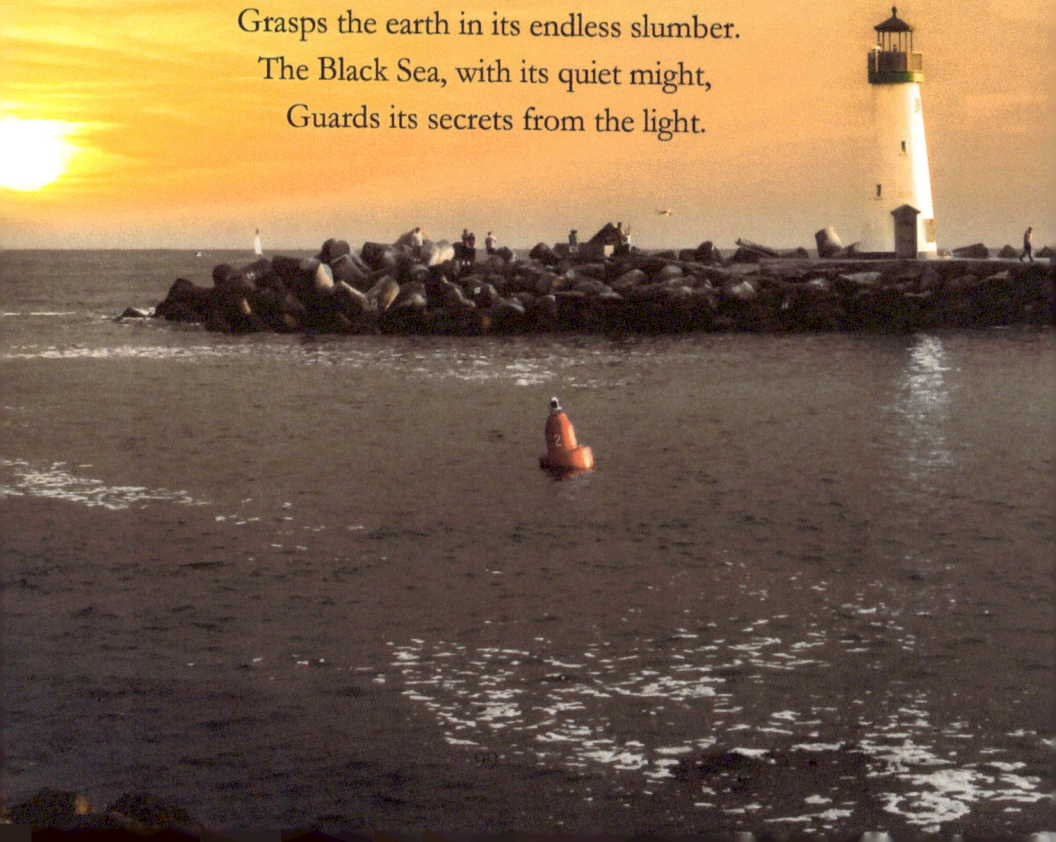

Star Sea

The oceansleeps,a canvas vast,
Where inky depths hold secrets cast.
With no moon in sight, the stars ignite,
A million jewels light up the night.
In the depths where the waters are clear,
The coral reef thrives, year after year.
Anemones bloom, and urchins crawl,
The reef, a living tapestry for all.
As night falls, the reef's pulse does not cease,
In the quiet dark, its wonders increase.
Glowing with life, in the ocean's deep,
The coral reef's secrets, it does keep.

SANCTUARY POEMS

POEMS OF REJUVENATION

New Beginnings Monitor National Marine Sanctuary

My excitement I can't contain
Forever for you my love remains
I'll work to keep you true
Longevity I long for me and you to
last, prosper and grow
Rewards we'll gather as we go.

Ancient wisdom

Thunder Bay National Marine Sanctuary

Banks of knowledge

From days of old

This is ancient wisdom

At least that's what I'm told

Vast understanding needing to know

For health and prosperity is my goal

Wisconson Shipwreck Coast

Wisconsin a parking lotunderthe sea

Maybe up to seven hundred stalls

Potentially there might be.

Two hundred Ship wrecks they seem to believe

This is a sailors museum without a doubt I Guarantee.

Just imagine all the treasures down deep to see.

Countless divers and explorers believe there are

Valuables beyond belief

Confront-Face the Stone

Gray's Reef National Marine Sanctuary

Gazing imagining while facing the stone

Creative, relative

I must be Dreams of no limit to set me free

A determined will, this is for me

Years Gone By

Florida Keys National Marine Sanctuary

Mixed color of meadows displayed

Arrayed beauty matured and aged

Times of past you wear so well

Magnified opulence is your story to tell

In the Moment

Flower Garden Banks National Marine Sanctuary

Flowers I see slow down taking

My time is the key What radiant majesty they

are Strolling with ease without a care

Enveloping beauty near and far

Lake Ontario

Niagara Falls you stand so tall

With walls of f360 feet that's gall

You are shaped like a queen

Like the great North American Beauty

With your borders touching New York

Canadian and the list goes on and on.

You flow as the world which you show

With an expression a Great Lake you glow

You reach far covering almost to Michigan

The whole nation even that motor city

And so much more

Escalation

Gerry E. Studds Stellwagen N/M.S

Celebrate friends, family

Support for our surrounding
Make the future bright

For yourself someone else and others

Nurture

Hawaiian Island Humpback Whale

National Marine Sanctuary

We feast, rest, nurturing the soul

Encouraging growth from birth till we grow old
Living , loving and learning
Is my number one goal
As these things continue
Will fantastic I know
Life to be

Soaring

Olympic Coast National Marine Sanctuary

I reach for hope aspiring for height

Ambitions to the stratosphere

Climbing with extraordinary might

Longing to make it yes we can

Soaring into the future

With abundance of plans

Monitor

Monterey Bay National Marine Sanctuary

Earth ocean sky and we
Are one for each other
For true harmony to be
Support for us all
Help we must give

Rest

Cordell Bank National Marine Sanctuary

I long to encompass your embrace

Upon my soul at peace offshore
Resting on islands of tranquil waters
At last restore rejuvenation renewal

Joy awaits me I know

Enjoy

Gulf of the Farallones National Marine Sanctuary

Like the birds they gather

And fly filling the waters & sky

Yes I feel like the sky

Joy, life thrilled oh my

To have joy, liberty the pursuit of happiness

Wise

Northwestern Hawaiian Islands Coral

SeaTurtles

You are wise as knowledge is gathered

Aged and weighed of the past used as

Guidance for today

Care for those that we see in need

Challenges

Fagatele Bay National Marine Sanctuary

Facing a chance to make me grow

From where will my strength come

Yes above and below

I know I'll make it stronger this time

From friends, neighbors, and the great divine

Remember the Past

Channel Island National Marine Sanctuary

Kelp forest a place providing pondering.

Protections for on going future and the
Past life it gives reflection of yester years

Directions amidst Our vast domain

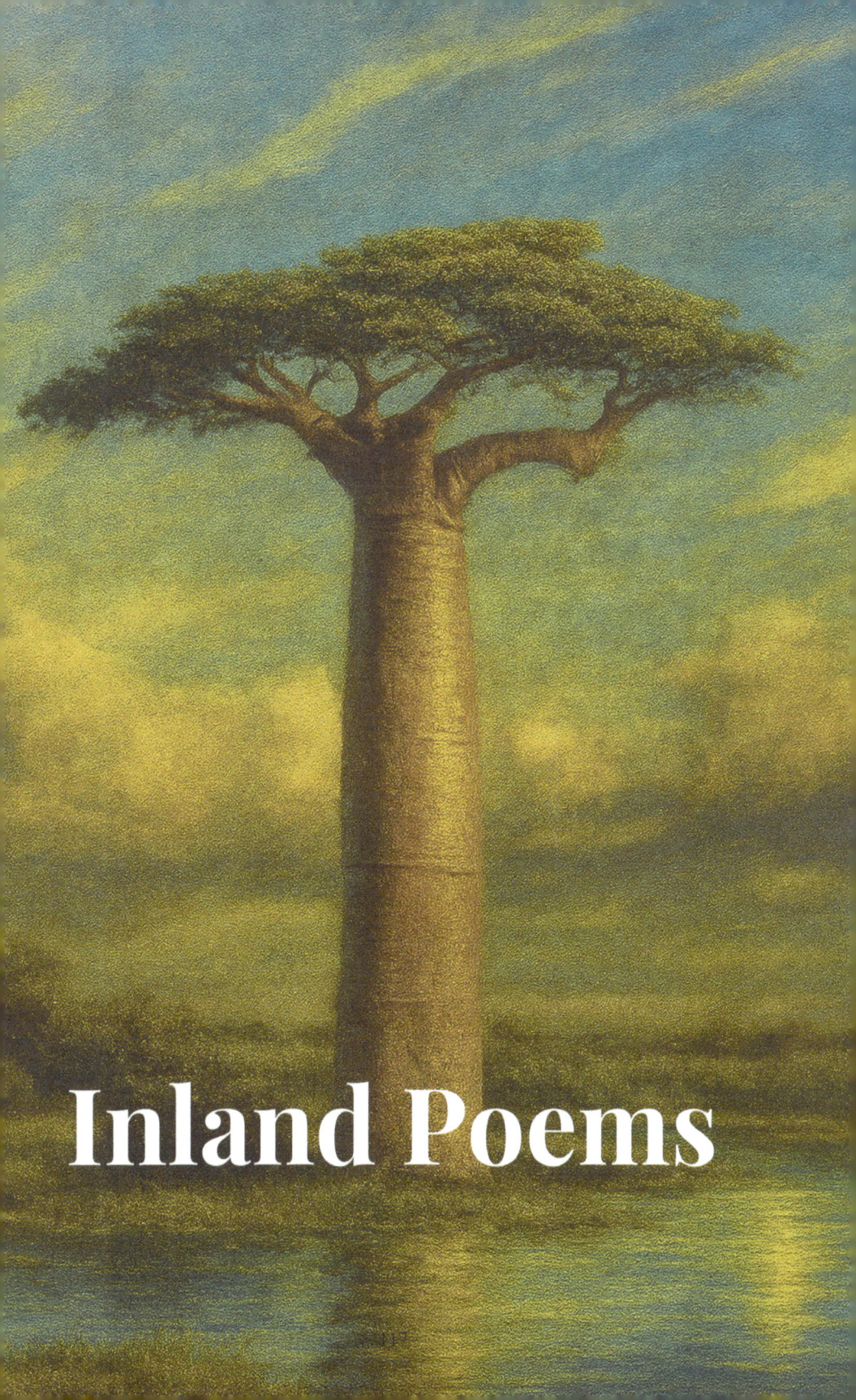

Inland Poems

Inland's to the Sea

From gutters to runoffs, from rain-fed streams,
Through dancing creeks and flowered dreams—
They wind through farms, they swell in ponds,

They rage through lakes with purpose strong.
Each ripple flows, each current weaves,
Into the rivers, onward to seas.

You're not alone—you're part of this tide.
An umbilical cord where waters abide.
From mountain trickle to ocean's roar,
We're bound by waters that came before.

So pause and ponder what you pour—
Each drop, each act, opens a door.
Choose with care, let kindness be.
For every choice shapes what flows free.

Inseparable Journey – Honey Bee

How sweet the flight, the humble bee,

A golden thread from land to sea.

You dance through blossoms, shore to shore,

A vital force, and so much more.

From inland valleys rich and wide,

You gift the world with nature's pride.

A silent builder, bold and small,

You weave the web that feeds us all.

Through trees, through skies, through winds that sing,

You touch the pulse of everything.

Your path connects both man and tree—

A bond of breath and unity.

So let our hearts not miss a beat,

Until our efforts are complete.

For in your flight, we clearly see

The future's hope—from land to sea.

Sahel

The Niger flows through dust and flame,
Its crusted banks still bear the name
Of sails that rose and dipped below,
As traders rowed with rhythmic flow.
Gold once glistened in desert light,
Crossing dunes from day to night.
From cargoed hulls to distant lands,
It slipped like secrets through the sands.
A king rode forth with wealth untold,
Camels crowned in silk and gold.
His legacy, a shining tale—
The world stood still, the skies grew pale.
Three kingdoms strong, their spirits blend,
In echoes time cannot suspend.
The river speaks, its waters cast
Reflections of a regal past.
Hear ye, hear ye—dawn draws near,
The river's mouth begins to cheer.
From mountain springs to ocean's tide,
Through ancient towns where hopes reside.
Take our anchor, call us kin—
Let friendship sail and journeys begin.
Through mighty currents wide and free,
We seek the soul within the sea.

Forked Deer River

I saw the sea in Tennessee,
Where Forked Deer flows wild and free.
Bullfrogs leapt from muddy banks,
In twilight's hush, through cypress ranks.

I heard the roar of Cumberland's might,
Where barges glided into night.
From deep within, a voice rang clear—
I rose to cast away my fear.

Down the Mississippi, bold and wide,
With dreams and cargo side by side,
Each bend, each wave, a whispered plea,
A path of purpose to the sea.

And westward still, my spirit steered,
Beyond the doubts I once had feared
Toward coastal winds, where skies expand—
I found my freedom in that land.

Ocean Health Benefits

Introduction

The ocean has long been recognized for its therapeutic properties, offering a unique combination of physical, mental, and emotional benefits. For many, it's a place of peace and rejuvenation, but for some, like myself, it has also become a source of healing and vitality. My relationship with the ocean goes beyond admiration for its beauty—it's rooted in personal health transformations.

I've always felt a strong attraction to the ocean, often finding solace in long walks on the beach and dipping my feet in the water. Living in landlocked Tennessee, I never quite understood why this connection felt so natural. It wasn't until I moved to California that I began to fully appreciate the ocean's impact on my health. After years of struggling with sinus issues in Tennessee's humid climate, the fresh, salty air of the coast cleared up my nasal passages significantly. But my journey didn't end there.

Following a diagnosis of kidney disease, I learned that ocean water supports cell regeneration, which can benefit kidney function. This discovery drove me to the water, where I began to immerse myself—literally and figuratively—in the ocean's healing powers. The ocean, once simply a place of beauty, has now become a crucial part of my wellness routine, much like nutritious food for the body and mind.

Today, as a former marketer with a background in business and media, Iproudly consider myself an "Oceanic Marketer," passionate about sharing the lifeenhancing benefits the ocean offers.

The ocean's healing powers are as vast as its waters. From respiratory relief to enhanced mental wellbeing, here are 30 ways the ocean can benefit your health:

30 Ocean Health Benefits

1. Boosts Respiratory Health

Salty air near the ocean is rich in negativeions, which help cleanse the respiratory system by clearing the lungs and improving lung function. Negative ions can neutralize airborne pollutants and allergens, making breathing easier for individuals with conditions like asthma, bronchitis, or chronic obstructive pulmonary disease (COPD).

2. Improves Skin Health

Ocean water contains a high concentration of minerals like magnesium, calcium, and potassium, which can rejuvenate and nourish the skin. These minerals help the skin retain moisture, reducing dryness and irritation. Saltwater also has natural antiseptic properties, helping to cleanse the skin of bacteria and toxins, making it an effective remedy for skin conditions such as eczema, psoriasis, and acne. Regular exposure to seawater can leave the skin smoother and clearer.

3. Promotes Relaxation and Reduces Stress

The rhythmic sound of ocean waves, along with the vast visual expanse of the sea, creates a natural calming effect on the brain. This soothing "white noise" helps lower cortisol levels, the body's primary stress hormone, leading to reduced feelings of anxiety and promoting relaxation. Being near the ocean encourages mindfulness and a meditative state, helping individuals disconnect from daily stressors. Simply spending time by the shore can enhance mental wellbeing and promote emotional balance.

4. Increases Vitamin D Intake

Spending time at the beachor by the ocean means more exposure to natural sunlight, which stimulates the body's production of vitamin D. This essential nutrient plays a key role in bone health by aiding calcium absorption. Vitamin D is also vital for immune function, mood regulation, and hormone balance. Deficiency in this vitamin has been linked to depression, weakened immunity, and increased risk of chronic diseases. Regular visits to the ocean can help maintain optimal vitamin D levels, especially for those living in regions with limited sunlight.

5. Improves Circulation

Walking in shallow ocean water can improve blood circulation throughout the body. The cool temperature of the water stimulates blood flow, helping to oxygenate tissues and organs. Physical movement along the beach also increases heart rate, promoting better cardiovascular health. This gentle form of exercise boosts energy levels and supports the body's natural healing processes.

6. Supports Weight Loss

Ocean based activities such as walking on the beach or along the shoreline provide excellent opportunities for calorie burning, lowimpact exercise. Walking in sand requires more effort than walking on solid ground, increasing energy expenditure and promoting fat loss. These activities also engage various muscle groups, making beach walks effective for weight management and cardiovascular fitness.

7. Alleviates Joint Pain

The buoyancy of seawater creat a lowimpact environment f physical activity, reducing t strain on joints and muscles. F individuals with arthritis or joi pain, this buoyancy allows for greater range of motion ar mobility without causi discomfort. Water's natu resistance can help build musc strength while reducing joi stress. This makes ocean exerci especially beneficial for tho with chronic pain, as it promot gentle movement while easir inflammation and stiffness.

8. Natural Detoxification

The highsalt content in oce water encourages detoxification drawing out impurities from t skin through osmosis. Simp walking barefoot in the water on wet sand helps open yo pores and remove toxins from t body, leaving your skin feelir refreshed. Seawater also suppor lymphatic drainage, promoting t body's natural detox processes.

9. Aids in Muscle Recovery

Cold oceanwater can help reduce muscle soreness and inflammation after physic activity. Walking in the ocean or immersing yourself briefly in cold seawater c provide a natural cooling effect, reducing the buildup of lactic acid in muscles ar speeding up recovery time. Athletes and fitness enthusiasts often use ocean wat for its muscle recovery benefits.

10. Reduces Inflammation

Sea water is rich in magnesium, a mineral known for its antiinflammatory properties. Regular exposure to magnesium can help reduce inflammation in the body, especially in joints and muscles. This makes seawater beneficial for people with conditions like arthritis, tendonitis, and muscle soreness. The antiinflammatory effects of ocean water help decrease pain and swelling, improve joint mobility, and enhance physical comfort.

11. Boosts the Immune System

Seawatercontains essential mineralslike potassium, iodine, and magnesium, which help boost immune function. Even standing in shallow ocean water or wading along the shore can increase your body's absorption of these minerals. Additionally, the fresh, salty air by the coast can strengthen the immune system by increasing the production of white blood cells, which are key to defending the body against infections.

12. Improves Digestion

Ocean water contains chloride, a mineral that plays a crucial role in the production of stomach acid, aiding digestion. While swimming is not required to benefit from this, small amounts of seawater inadvertently ingested during playful wading or walking in the ocean can support digestive health. The fresh coastal air, full of negative ions, also promotes gut health by relieving stress, which often disrupts digestion.

13. Supports Cardiovascular Health

Waling on the beach, especically in wet sand or shallow water, provides a gentle yet effective cardiovascular workout. The resistance from the sand and water challenges your muscles and heart, promoting better circulation and reducing blood pressure. Even a leisurely walk along the oceanfront can have significant benefits for heart health, as it encourages movement without putting too much strain on the body.

4. Enhances Balance and Coordination

Water sports like surfing, paddle boarding, and snorkeling require balance, coordination, and agility. These activities engage core muscles and help improve stability, balance, and overall motor skills. Regularly participating in these ocean activities strengthens the body's proprioceptive abilities (the sense of body positioning), which is beneficial for maintaining physical coordination, especially as people age.

15. Stimulates Acupuncture Points

Walking barefoot on wet sand or wading in ocean water stimulates reflexology points on the feet, much like acupuncture. This natural stimulation promotes blood flow, reduces tension, and encourages relaxation. The sensation of walking on sand or in seawater also engages various pressure points, which can improve circulation and overall physical wellbeing.

16. Natural Exfoliation

Walkingonsandy beaches actsas a natural exfoliant for your feet and skin. The friction from sand helps remove dead skin cells, leaving the skin smoother and refreshed. Unlike chemical exfoliants, sand provides a gentle, all natural way to rejuvenate the skin, improving its texture and appearance.

17. Helps Reduce Anxiety

Seawatercontains magnesium, which has a calming effect on the nervous system. Magnesium helps regulate stress and anxiety by lowering cortisol levels and increasing relaxation. Simply being near the ocean promotes mental clarity and peace, making it an ideal natural remedy for managing anxiety and improving emotional wellbeing.

18. Encourages Physical Activity

The ocean naturally encourages an active lifestyle by offering a wide range of recreational activities, including swimming, surfing, beach volleyball, and walking. Engaging in these outdoor activities not only benefits physical health but also enhances mental health by reducing stress and promoting social interaction.

19. Stimulates Cell Regeneration

Theminerals in seawater, such as iodine and sodium, play a vital role in promoting cell regeneration. These minerals help repair damaged skin and tissues, supporting healing processes for injuries and surgeries. Additionally, seawater's healing properties promote internal regeneration, which is beneficial for maintaining healthy organs and tissues.

20. Strengthens Bones

Exposure to sunlightnear theocean increases the body's production of vitamin D, which is essential for calcium absorption and bone strength. Regular exposure to vitamin D can help prevent osteoporosis and improve bone density, reducing the risk of fractures and bonerelated conditions.

21. Seaweed as a Superfood

Seaweed, particularly varieties like Nori, Wakame, and Kelp, is a nutrient dense superfood packed with essential vitamins, minerals, and antioxidants. Seaweed is rich in iodine, which is critical for proper thyroid function, helping regulate metabolism and hormonal balance. It also contains iron, calcium, magnesium, and fiber, supporting healthy digestion and preventing constipation. Seaweed's antioxidant properties help fight free radicals, reducing oxidative stress and potentially lowering the risk of chronic diseases like cancer. Regular consumption of seaweed can also support cardiovascular health by lowering cholesterol levels.

22. Omega3 Benefits from Fish

Fatty fish like salmon, mackerel, sardines,and tuna are among the best sources of Omega3 fatty acids, which provide significant health benefits. Omega3s, particularly DHA and EPA, are essential for maintaining heart health by reducing inflammation, lowering blood pressure, and decreasing triglycerides. They also support brain function, improving cognitive performance, memory, and mood. Regular consumption of Omega3rich fish has been shown to reduce the risk of heart disease, stroke, and neurodegenerative diseases such as Alzheimer's. In addition, e Omega 3 rich. help reduce joint pain and stiffness, making them beneficial for individuals with arthritis.

23. Sea Moss for Immune Support

Sea moss (also known as Irish moss) is a popular superfood that is rich in vitamins and minerals such as zinc, iodine, potassium, and magnesium, all of which support immune function. Sea moss has been used traditionally as a natural remedy to strengthen the immune system and ward off colds, flu, and infections. Its high antioxidant content helps fight free radicals, protecting cells from oxidative damage. Sea moss is also known for its antiinflammatory properties, which can reduce inflammation throughout the body, promoting faster recovery from illness. Additionally, it is a natural prebiotic that supports gut health, which is closely linked to immune function.

24. Fish Oil for Joint Health

Fishoil, extracted from fatty fish like salmon, is a concentrated source of Omega3 fatty acids, which are highly beneficial for joint health. Omega3s help reduce inflammation in the joints, improving symptoms of arthritis and other inflammatory conditions. Studies have shown that regular consumption of fish oil can decrease morning stiffness, tenderness, and swelling in individuals with rheumatoid arthritis. Omega3s also promote joint lubrication, making movement easier and reducing wear and tear on cartilage. Fish oil supplements are widely used to support mobility, especially among older adults or those engaged in physical activities that strain the joints.

25. Seaweed for Detoxification

Certain types of seaweed, especially brown seaweed like wakame and kombu, have natural detoxifying properties. They contain alginate, a compound that helps bind to heavy metals and toxins in the digestive tract, preventing them from being absorbed into the bloodstream. This makes seaweed an excellent addition to detox diets, as it supports the body's natural elimination processes. Seaweed is also high in fiber, promoting healthy digestion and regular bowel movements, which further helps remove waste and toxins from the body. Regular consumption of seaweed can aid in liver function and contribute to overall detoxification.

26. Sea Moss for Skin Health

Sea moss is renowned for its benefits to the skin. Rich in collagen boosting nutrients like vitamin C and amino acids, sea moss promotes skin elasticity, hydration, and firmness. It is often used in skin care products due to its ability to enhance the skin's natural moisture barrier, reducing dryness and promoting a healthy glow. Sea moss also contains antimicrobial properties, which can help reduce acne and prevent skin infections. When ingested, its high nutrient content helps improve overall skin health from the inside out, making it a natural remedy for various skin conditions.

27. Electromagnetic Benefits from Full Moons

The ocean is deeply influenced by the gravitational pull of the moon, particularly during full moons when tides rise and fall dramatically. Some research suggests that these gravitational and electromagnetic shifts may have subtle effects on human health, especially for those living near the coast. During full moons, people often report better sleep, enhanced mental clarity, and a greater sense of calm, potentially linked to circadian rhythms and tidal influences. The body's natural biofield, which responds to electromagnetic forces, may be positively affected by the fluctuations in the Earth's magnetic field caused by these lunar cycles, although more research is needed to fully understand these effects.

28. Cold Water Immersion Benefits

Coldocean water immersion stimulates the production of cold shock proteins, which help protect cells and support the body's ability to recover from stress or injury. Cold water triggers a survival response in the body, causing blood vessels to constrict, which reduces swelling and inflammation. This process also promotes faster muscle recovery and helps reduce pain in individuals with inflammatory conditions. Regular exposure to cold water has been linked to enhanced circulation, improved immune function, and an increase in metabolic rate.

29. Fish for Cognitive Function

Consuming fatty fish like salmon is highly beneficial for cognitive health due to its high content of DHA, an Omega3 fatty acid essential for brain structure and function. DHA is a major component of brain cell membranes and is crucial for maintaining cognitive performance, memory, and mental clarity. Regular consumption of DHA-rich fish has been associated with a reduced risk of Alzheimer's disease and cognitive decline. Fish also contains vitamin B12 and selenium, which contribute to brain health and help protect against neurological disorders. Omega3s from fish support neuron health and improve neurotransmitter function, making fish a powerful brain food.

30. Seaweed for Weight Management

The fiber content in seaweed, particularly soluble fiber like alginate, can he regulate appetite and promote satiety, making it an excellent food for weig management. Seaweed also contains a compound called fucoxanthin, which h been shown to increase fat metabolism and promote weight loss by encouraging t body to burn stored fat. Additionally, the low calorie, nutrient dense profile seaweed makes it a healthy addition to any diet, providing essential nutrien without excess calories. Seaweed is often used in detox and weight loss diets for ability to support digestion, boost metabolism, and improve nutrient absorption.

Oceanic Rhythm and Patterns

Knowledge Is Like The Vastness Of TheOcean— EverExpanding,Deep,andFullof UntappedPotential.

KNOWLEDGE AND UNDERSTANDING are like the tides ,essential forces that guide you toward success. Without them, just as a sailor without a compass, your potential can never be fully reached.

This booklet offers thirty activating concepts, one for each day of the month, that will help you navigate through life's challenges, empowering you to excel in all areas.

There are rhythms and patterns in all living things, much like the currents and waves of the ocean. Discover yours, flow with them, and allow them to propel you forward. Your personal rhythms and patterns act as both a roadmap and fuel, directing your path and providing the energy needed to reach your life's destination.

As the ocean ebbs and flows, so too should your commitment to self improvement. Start by reading this booklet through in one uninterrupted sitting to absorb the concepts fully. Review the exercises and determine which ones align with your needs. It's recommended to walk for at least twenty minutes daily, much like the waves continuously shaping the shoreline.

Each morning, as you awaken, read one concept. Reflect on it, and allow it to guide your actions throughout the day, much like a captain who adjusts their course to the winds. Incorporate the day's concept into your daily activities, and remember to take a twenty minute walk — before work, during lunch, or after, whatever best suits your schedule. At night, revisit the day's concept before you sleep, letting it settle in your mind like the peaceful rhythm of the tide. The next day, move on to the following concept and follow the same routine.

After completing all thirty concepts in a month, you will find yourself exercising both body and mind. Then, begin again from the start.

Follow through with this practice day by day, month by month, and after a full year, stand back and admire your progress, much like gazing over the horizon after a long journey at sea. You will be amazed by how much you have grown, how your life has transformed, and how well you've navigated your path to success.

Day 1: Visualize Who You Want to Be

Just as the ocean molds the shoreline over time, so too can you shape your life through the power of visualization. Whatever you can see clearly in your mind, you can bring into existence. Whoever you wish to become, you can create, just as the ocean's currents carve paths through the waters.

Be true to yourself — become the person you are meant to be in every respect: in character, integrity, spirituality, creativity, career, finances, and in the eyes of those you love and those who admire you.

Picture yourself as the person you dream of being, like a ship navigating toward a distant horizon. Visualize yourself living the life you desire, carrying out the work you are passionate about, interacting with others with kindness and generosity, just as the ocean sustains life in all its depths. Envision your ability to love and care for those closest to you, your support and leadership in your community, and your growth in morality, ethics, and compassion.

The ocean covers over 70% of the Earth's surface, making it one of the most vast and mysterious places on the planet. Like the ocean, your potential is immense—once you start exploring, there are endless possibilities.

Day 2: Set Goals

Now that you have charted a course through visualization, it's time to set your goals — your guiding stars — that will lead you to your destination.

As you reflected yesterday on the person you want to become, did certain ideas surface on how to reach that vision? The more you focus on your desired self, the clearer your plans become. Which of the many steps should come first? Can some be pursued together? Which ones need time to develop?

Setting goals is like following a well planned route on the open sea. Determine the time it will take and the actions required, but approach each step with positivity and joy, knowing that the journey itself is part of your success.

Sea turtles move thousands of miles across the ocean to reach their nesting grounds, demonstrating the power of setting a destination.

Day 3: Create A Creative Environment

In your home, carve out a space that nurtures your creativity and focus, just as a tide pool nurtures life with its calm, shallow waters. Furnish this space with tools that facilitate your creativity: a comfortable chair, a well lit desk, and a notebook or journal where you can chart your progress. Keep this space free from distractions and surround yourself with items that inspire you. Consider adding a cork board where you can pin up pictures of loved ones or role models Keep this space uncluttered, for clutter disrupts the natural flow of creativity, just as debris in the ocean hinders a smooth sail.

Coral reefs, often called the "rainforests of the sea," create vibrant ecosystems that support countless species. A creative environment fosters growth in the same way—nurture your space, and creativity will flourish.

Day 4: Create a Plan and Write It Down

Writing down your goals is of paramount importance — it helps you understand how to move forward with precision and direction. Your plan will serve as your guide, ensuring that you stay on course.

Start by writing freely, capturing your thoughts like the diverse life forms in the open ocean. Then, refine these ideas.

By organizing your thoughts into a clear plan, you are creating a powerful map that will guide you toward success. Embrace this process as an opportunity to bring your goals to life, much like the ocean's currents bring nutrients to sustain life across vast distances.

Ocean currents follow predictable patterns, like the Gulf Stream, helping ships navigate efficiently across the sea.

Day 5: Find Your Rhythms and Patterns

Just as the tides ebb and flow with perfect rhythm, so too do our bodies and minds follow natural patterns. These rhythms, known as circadian rhythms, affect all living creatures, guiding when we are most alert, energetic, or in need of rest.

You may already be aware of your rhythms: perhaps you are sharpest in the early morning, much like the refreshing calm of the ocean at dawn. Or perhaps you find your energy builds later in the evening.

If you haven't paid attention to these cycles, now is the time to observe them. Keep a diary to note your peak hours and your low times, much like tracking the phases of the tides. Use this knowledge to fuel your goals. When you align your tasks with your natural rhythms, you'll find that reaching your destination becomes much smoother.

The tides are caused by the gravitational pull of the moon and follow a regular rhythm. Understanding the rhythms of the ocean can help predict its behavior

Day 6: Get an Attitude — A Positive One

A positive attitude is like the ocean breeze that fills your sails and propel you forward. When faced with new ideas or suggestions, how do you respond? If your instinct is to react negatively, you may be closing yourself off from exciting new adventures, opportunities, or connections.

Negativity doesn't breed growth, much like stagnant water doesn't support life. Practice developing a habit of seeing the positive side of situations, much like how sunlight breaks through clouds over the sea. This doesn't mean you must agree with everything, but rather approach each situation with an open and clear mind, free from negativity.

At first, adoptinotive attitude may feel unnatural, but with practice, i will become second nature. Remember, a positive attitude attracts good things into your life.

Dolphins are known for their playful and positive attitude in the ocean. Studies have shown that dolphins use teamwork and positivity to thrive in their environment.

Day 7: Build Faith and Commitment

The faith and commitment must remain unwavering at all times even when challenges arise. Let go of instant distrust and jealousy, for these emotions cloud your judgment.

Like a lighthouse standing tall amidst turbulent seas, your trust and commitment to your loved ones, friends, and colleagues will shine through and be rewarded. Though deception may come from a few, do not let it turn you cynical or skeptical.

Faith is like an anchor, keeping you grounded, and commitment is like the ocean's tides — steady, dependable, and essential to the rhythm of life.

Whales travel thousands of miles every year to breed and feed, staying committed to their migratory patterns.

Day 8: Knowing You Can Change Brings Freedom

The sea, with its ebb and flow, reminds us that stagnation is not an option — everything evolves, whether it's the tides, the shoreline, or your own journey.

When you allow yourself to grow spiritually, intellectually, and emotionally, you break free from limitations. Reflect on the changes that have occurred in your life. Did they lead to growth because you were open to them? Did you embrace them like the ocean embraces the changing seasons? If past changes didn't serve you, ask yourself why. Were you holding onto the shore when you should have been riding the wave?

Give yourself permission to change and grow. This freedom will bring you closer to your true self, allowing you to move forward with purpose and grace.

The ocean is constantly changing, with new species being discovered and ecosystems adapting. Scientists believe that 91% of marine life have yet to be identified.

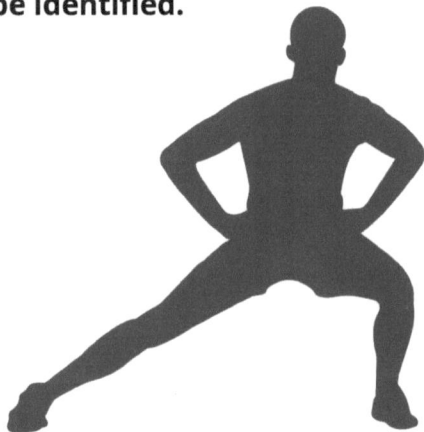

Day 9: Banish Fear by Being in the Present

By being mindful, you can banish fear from your life, much like how the sun's rays dissolve the morning mist over the sea.

Focus entirely on the task before you, whether it's a conversation, reading a book, or working on a goal. Being fully present allows you to navigate through life with clarity and confidence.

At first, your mind may drift like a boat without an anchor, but with practice, you will stay grounded in the moment. Fear has no space to grow in a mind that is fully engaged.

When you can release fear, you move forward boldly, like a ship breaking through the waves, confident in your direction and ready to embrace life's adventures with joy.

Sharks are known for their laser focus and presence in the moment when hunting. By staying fully present, they become apex predators.

Day 10: Know That an Unseen Power Is There to Help You

The ocean is filled with unseen forces — from powerful underwater currents to the gravitational pull of the moon guiding the tides. These forces, though invisible, shape the movement of the seas, just as unseen powers can guide you through life's uncertainties.

Trust in this unseen energy, whether it's your inner strength, intuition or a higher force. Just as marine animals like whales rely on the magnetic fields of the Earth to navigate across vast distances, you too have an inner compass guiding you toward your purpose.

When obstacles arise, remember that unseen forces are at work, much like the currents beneath the ocean's surface. Trust in these forces to steer you in the right direction, even when the path ahead is unclear.

Deep ocean currents, which are invisible on the surface, regulate climate and bring lifegiving nutrients to the ocean.

Day 11: Love and Live Life — Give a Smile Away

This is one of the easiest exercises you will ever do: As soon as you give a smile away, you will have it returned to you. When you smile in greeting, you make the recipient feel special and welcome. Barriers often break down at the "onslaught" of a smile. When you smile, you can't feel sad. Think of something pleasant, and smile right now. When a friend calls, greet them with joy, making them feel valued and important. Over time, this practice will become natural, and you'll find that it brightens not just your day, but others' as well.

Just like the tides of the ocean that are in constant motion, always giving and returning, your smile can create a ripple effect, reaching others and coming back to you, creating a sense of warmth and connection.

Seahorses are known for their gentle, peaceful nature, and they even smile in their own way.

Day 12: Practice Listening as You Would Practice a Sport

Listening, like navigating the ocean, requires skill and patience. Just as sailors must attune themselves to the rhythm of the sea, you must tune in to the rhythm of conversation. Listen with full attention, just as you would practice and refine a sport—improving with time and dedication.

When someone speaks, lean in as the ocean listens to the pull of the moon, affecting its tides. Your body language, like the calm waters of a serene bay, should reflect openness and receptivity. Be mindful of folding your arms or looking away—this can create barriers, much like a sudden storm disrupts a smooth voyage.

True listening, like the ocean absorbing the whispers of the wind, brings clarity and connection. The more you practice, the more natural it becomes, and like the ocean, your ability to listen will create harmony and flow in your relationships.

Whales communicate through long, complex songs that travel for miles across the ocean. By listening carefully to one another, they stay connected across vast distances. Listening is a powerful tool, just like whale songs.

Day 13: What You Give in a Relationship You Will Receive

The ocean provides for all forms of life, nourishing them with its bounty, and in return, the life it sustains helps maintain its balance. Similarly, in relationships, what you give—respect, kindness, and understanding—will come back to you, fostering mutual growth and harmony.

Just as the ocean is a source of life, your actions toward others can be a source of positivity and support. Treat others as you would want to be treated, and your relationships will thrive, like the interconnected ecosystems within a coral reef.

Think of each interaction as an opportunity to plant seeds of compassion and understanding, much like how the ocean's currents spread nutrients to nourish life. The care you give will circle back to you, ensuring your relationships remain strong and fulfilling.

Coral reefs provide shelter and nutrients to countless marine species, and in return, those species protect and feed the coral.

Day 14: Share Your Ideas with Supportive People

You should surround yourself with people who will uplift and encourage your ideas. Share your thoughts with those who will listen with care, much like the ocean supports countless forms of life, each dependent on the other for survival.

When you speak openly with trusted friends, mentors, or colleagues, you create a network of support—much like the interconnected coral reefs that sustain marine ecosystems. Your ideas, when nurtured in a positive environment, will grow stronger and more vibrant.

Remember that even the vast ocean is supported by unseen forces, such as tides and currents. Surround yourself with people who provide that same unseen strength, guiding and helping you navigate through life's challenges.

Schools of fish move together in harmony, creating safety and success through collective effort.

Day 15: Find a True Mentor

Finding a mentor can provide you with the wisdom and support you need to succeed. A mentor, like a lighthouse on a foggy coastline, helps illuminate your path, showing you the way when the waters become unclear.

Seek out someone who has navigated the challenges you face. Their experience will help you stay on course and avoid unnecessary detours. In the same way that marine animals travel with the guidance of nature's currents, you can advance more quickly and confidently with a mentor by your side.

Express gratitude for their guidance, as the ocean thanks the moon for its constant pull on the tides. A mentor's influence can help you achieve great things, just as the currents help marine life reach distant shores.

Baby sea turtles rely on the stars and the moon to guide them to the ocean after hatching.

Day 16: Take a Good Look at Yourself

The ocean, with its clear surface and deep waters, invites reflection In the same way, take a moment to observe yourself as if you were looking into a calm sea. Are you content with the person you see both inside and out?

Like the ocean's ability to shape its shores, you have the power to shape your life. If your outer appearance doesn't reflect the healthy confident person you aspire to be, make the necessary changes, just as waves gradually reshape the coastline.

Look within, too. Can you see the goodness, integrity, and strength you wish to project? If not, cultivate these qualities—just as the ocean sustains life below its surface. The deeper you look, the more you will discover your true self, ready to emerge and thrive.

The clarity of the ocean's water depends on how many particles are suspended in it.

Day 17: The Electricity of Teamwork

The ocean is filled with invisible energy, from the electrical impulses guiding schools of fish to the currents that sustain entire ecosystems. Teamwork operates in much the same way, with each person contributing to the shared energy that drives success.

Have you ever been stuck on a problem, only to find that when you talk it over with a teammate, the solution suddenly appears? This is the electricity of teamwork at play—an exchange of ideas and energy that leads to breakthroughs.

When you collaborate with others, your combined energy, much like the ocean's waves, will help you accomplish far more than you could on your own.

Some species of fish, like the electric eel, use electrical currents to communicate and sense their surroundings.

Day 18: Networking is the Way to Go

In the ocean survival often depnds on interconnected relationships. Marine life thrives in ecosystems where each species contributes to the whole. In the same way, networking can help you grow both personally and professionally

Join groups or communities that align with your goals, much like different species in a coral reef rely on one another. By participating in these networks, you can tap into new resources, share knowledge, and gain support from others who share your vision.

Remember, just as marine animals form symbiotic relationships, your connections will enrich your life and help you achieve your dreams. Networking is a powerful tool—use it to build bridges and create a path toward your success.

Coral reefs thrive due to the interconnected relationships between different species.

Day 19: Create Harmony — Banish Stress

The ocean, with its rhythmic waves and tranquil beauty, is a symbol of balance and harmony. Just as the sea calms our senses, you can create harmony in your life by embracing moments of peace and reflection.

Take time each day to reconnect with nature, whether it's a walk along the shore or simply observing the gentle ebb and flow of the tides. The ocean's timeless rhythm can remind you to slow down, breathe deeply, and banish stress from your life.

Let the beauty of the natural world inspire calm and gratitude, helping you navigate life's challenges with ease.

The rhythmic sound of ocean waves has a calming effect on the human brain, often reducing stress.

Day 20: Exercise

Just as theocean never ceases its movement, your body thrives when in motion. Regular exercise is essential for maintaining physical and mental wellbeing, much like how the constant flow of the tides keeps the ocean healthy and vibrant.

Incorporate daily movement—whether it's a walk along the beach, a swim in the sea, or a series of exercises at home. Each movement strengthens your body.

Exercise not only benefits your body but also your mind. Keep your body in motion, and you'll feel more energized, focused, and ready to take on life's challeng es.

Dolphins and many marine creatures must swim constantly to stay healthy and survive.

Day 21: Making Opportunities of Crises

Just as storms churn the ocean's surface, crises in life can feel overwhelming. But remember, after every storm, the sea returns to calm, and often, the turmoil brings new life and opportunities to the ocean's depths. Similarly, every crisis presents an opportunity for growth.

When faced with a crisis, take a moment to reflect on what could have been done differently. Like writing down a course for a ship, documenting the events leading up to the crisis can help you see clearly where things went astray. Then, focus on finding solutions, as the ocean finds balance after a disturbance.

Every crisis is a chance to overcome, just as marine life rebounds and thrives after a storm. By viewing crises as opportunities, you can grow stronger and more resilient, much like the ocean after the passing of turbulent waves.

After an oil spill, the ocean has an incredible ability to begin self healing with the help of bacteria that break down oil.

Day 22: Grow Intellectually and Spiritually

The ocean's mysteries are vast and endless, with scientists still discovering new species and ecosystems deep within its waters. Similarly, your potential for growth—intellectually and spiritually— knows no bounds.

Challenge yourself to explore new ideas and expand your knowledge, just as explorers dive into the ocean's depths in search of new discoveries. Read widely, learn new skills, and open your heart to spiritual growth.

Like the ocean currents that constantly circulate and bring fresh life to even the darkest depths, the flow of new knowledge and spiritual insight will refresh and energize your soul.

The deep ocean is one of the least explored areas on Earth. More than 80% of our ocean is unmapped, unexplored, and undiscovered.

Day 23: Incorporate Charity in Your Life

The ocean gives generously, sustainingcountless species with its resources, from the smallest plankton to thelargestwhales. Inyour life, too, charity and giving should be central themes.

When you help others, you create ripples that extend far beyond the initial act of kindness, much like how a drop of water expands across the surface of the sea. Charity isn't always about grand gestures; even tiny acts of kindness benefit the community and the globe as a whole, just as the ocean supports life at all levels.

Remember that, like the ocean, your capacity to give is vast, and the more you give, the more abundance you will receive in return. By emulating the ocean's generosity, you enrich not only the lives of others but also your own soul.

Many species of fish clean the skin of larger fish in a mutualistic relationship that benefits both.

Day 24: You Are a Valued Employee

The ocean plays a great role in the balance of life on Earth, much like you play an integral role in your workplace. Understand your value and work toward being a dependable, outstanding team member.

Just as marine animals like dolphins and orcas collaborate to hunt or play, you too should aim to work in harmony with your colleagues. Be thorough in your tasks, and approach your work with pride, knowing that your contribution, like a wave on the shore, has a lasting impact.

When you stand out as a reliable and valued employee, you create opportunities for growth and advancement, just as the ocean provides for the creatures that depend on it. Trust in your abilities, and you will continue to rise in your career, much like the tides that lift all boats.

In the ocean, every creature has a role to play, from the smallest plankton to the largest whale, contributing to the balance of the ecosystem.

Day 25: Create a Study Hour

The ocean, vast and filled with unknown depths,invites exploration,

much like your mind. To grow and reach your potential, dedicate time each day to study and reflection.

Just as explorers of the sea chart a course before embarking on a voyage, create a study plan and stick to it. Whether you're learning a new subject or deepening your understanding of a topic, approach it methodically. This dedicated time will be like navigating new waters, allowing you to gain knowledge and wisdom that will propel you toward your goals.

Think of the ocean's quiet depths, where life continues to evolve and flourish. Your mind, too, needs time for quiet reflection and study to expand your understanding of the world and yourself.

Octopuses and other marine animals are well known for their capacity to solve problems and learn via observation.

Day 26: Practice and Rehearse

Just asthe ocean'swaves practicetheirrhythmic dance against theshore day after day, so too should you practice and rehearse your goals. Repetition and refinement are the keys to mastery.

Stand before a mirror and speak your goals out loud, much like the waves echo their song across the beach. As you hear your voice affirming your desires, you'll strengthen your resolve and bring those dreams closer to reality. The more you practice, the more natural and confident you will become, much like the ocean never hesitates in its relentless motion.

The phrase "**To act the master is to become the master**" is like the ocean's mantra—constant, unwavering, and powerful. Practice with purpose, and soon you will find yourself mastering every goal you set.

Sea otters practice behaviors like cracking open shells on rocks to get better at it.

Day 27: Choose Words Wisely

Words are like the waves of the ocean—once spoken, they can carry immense power and reach far beyond their point of origin. Just as the waves can either nurture or erode the shoreline, your words can uplift or tear down.

Choose your words with care, knowing that they can create lasting impressions. Speak positively and thoughtfully, just as the ocean delivers nourishment through its currents. Words of encouragement and hope, like the ocean's gifts, can inspire others and lead to positive change in your life and the lives of those around you.

Remember, just as the ocean is vast and deep, so is the power of your words. Use them to create harmony, growth, and connection, and they will return to you in kind.

Whale songs are used for communication across vast distances in the ocean. These songs are carefully crafted and play an important role in their social structure.

Day 28: Make Decisions, Trust Intuition

The ocean's currents are often invisible, yet they guide marine life across vast distances with precision. In the same way, your intuition can act as an unseen guide, helping you make important decisions in life.

When faced with a choice, trust that inner voice—the current beneath the surface—that knows the right direction. Sometimes, like the ocean's tides, decisions need to be made quickly and decisively. Trust that your intuition, much like the instinctual migrations of sea creatures, will lead you on the right path.

Making decisions is like setting your sails to catch the wind; once you've chosen a direction, commit to it, and let your intuition guide you confidently toward your destination.

Sea creatures like crabs quickly adapt to changing tides and environmental conditions by instinct.

Day 29: Fiscal Responsibility

The ocean is vast, yet every drop of water is accounted for in the grand cycle of tides and currents. Similarly, you must be mindful of your resources and practice fiscal responsibility in your life.

Keep track of where your money goes, just as oceanographers monitor the flow of currents and tides. Create a budget, set financial goals, and live within your means. Save a part of your income to ensure you can weather any storms, much like how the ocean's ecosystems rely on reserves of nutrients to survive tough times.

Being responsible with your finances, like the ocean maintaining balance in its ecosystems, will provide you with stability and peace of mind. Financial discipline today leads to freedom and security tomorrow, just as the ocean's currents are always moving toward balance.

Hermit crabs move into new shells when they outgrow their old ones, demonstrating careful resource management.

Day 30: You Are What You Think

The ocean is shaped by powerful unseen forces—gravity, wind, and currents—that determine its tides, waves, and patterns. Likewise, your thoughts shape your reality. What you think, you become.

Let your thoughts be as vast and free as the ocean, open to all possibilities.

Feed your mind with positive, uplifting ideas, and watch these thoughts influence your actions and shape your world. Just as the ocean is always in motion, your thoughts should flow freely, guiding you toward your goals.

Bioluminescent creatures in the deep sea create their own light, illuminating the dark waters around them. A whopping 76% of all oceanic marine life are bioluminescent.

USA Oceanic Sanctuaries

The National Marine Sanctuary System of the United States

The National Marine Sanctuary System is a constellation of protected underwater parks administered by the Office of National Marine Sanctuaries (ONMS), which is a subdivision of the National Oceanic and Atmospheric Administration (NOAA), expanding across more than 620,000 square miles of marine and Great Lakes waters. Spanning from Washington State to the Florida Keys and from Lake Huron to American Samoa, this network includes 16 national marine sanctuaries along with the Papahānaumokuākea and Rose Atoll Marine National Monuments. Moreover, five more sanctuaries have been proposed in recent times.

1 Olympic Coast National Marine Sanctuary

Olympic Coast National Marine Sanctuary showcases one of North America's richest marine environments and untouched coastlines. Spanning 3,189 square miles off the Olympic Peninsula's rugged coast, this sanctuary safeguards diverse ecosystems, from kelp forests and intertidal zones to deepsea coral communities. Established in 1994, it also honors the cultural heritage of the region's Indigenous communities — the Hoh, Makah, Quileute, and Quinault—who have deep, lasting ties to the ocean. The sanctuary's mission focuses on protecting these natural and cultural treasures, preserving ecological integrity, and fostering public understanding through education.

2 Greater Farallones National Marine Sanctuary

Greater Farallones National Marine Sanctuary, established in 1981, originally covered 1,279 square miles but expanded in 2015 to over 3,200 square miles. Located along the California coast, this sanctuary is part of the productive California Current ecosystem. It supports a vibrant array of marine life, from endangered species like gray, blue, elephant seals, harbor seals, Stellar sea lions, Pacific white sided dolphins, and humpback whales to thriving populations of white sharks. The sanctuary's ecosystem is driven by nutrient rich waters brought to the surface by upwelling currents, making it one of the most biologically abundant regions worldwide.

3 Cordell Bank National Marine Sanctuary

Cordell Bank National Marine Sanctuary lies entirelyoffshore, covering 1,286 square miles of ocean, and was established in 1989. Located on the coast of California, It protects diverse habitats, including rocky banks, deepsea canyons, and soft seafloor ecosystems. This area serves as a vital feeding ground for seabirds, fish, and marine mammals. The remote location makes it an ideal site for scientific research, with sanctuary scientists working closely with universities and other partners to study this biodiverse region.

4 Monterey Bay National Marine Sanctuary

Often dubbed the "Serengeti of the Sea," Monterey Bay National Marine Sanctuary is a breathtaking stretch of over 6,000 sq miles along California's central coast. As a matter of fact, it is one of the largest sanctuary systems in the U.S., and it was founded in 1992. Encompassing tide pools, kelp forests, and underwater canyons, it is home to an incredible variety of marine life, from shrimp to majestic blue whales. The sanctuary also emphasizes environmental protection and public engagement, inviting visitors to explore its rich ecosystems and participate in preserving this national marine treasure.

5 Channel Islands National Park National Marine Sanctuary

The Channel Islands, often called the "Galapagos of North America," was established in 1980 and spans 1,470 square miles of ocean around five islands off the coast of Southern California. This protected area lies at the confluence of two major ocean currents, fostering incredible biodiversity, from kelp forests and deepsea coral habitats to endangered species and historic shipwrecks. The sanctuary's remote location preserves the unique ecosystems and rich cultural history of the Chumash people, who have lived in the area for thousands of years. It also supports various commercial and recreational activities like fishing and tourism while prioritizing conservation and sustainable use. Programs like

"Los Marineros" and "Students at Sea" engage the public in marine education, reinforcing the sanctuary's commitment to research, outreach, and the protection of natural and cultural resources.

6 Thunder Bay National Marine Sanctuary

Thunder Bay National Marine Sanctuary, situated in Lake Huron off the northeastern coast of Michigan, covers an expansive 4,300 square miles (11,000 km²) following its 2014 expansion. Founded in 2000, It plays a great role in preserving the region's maritime heritage, protecting around 116 historically significant shipwrecks that span from 19th century wooden vessels to 20th century steel steamers. The sanctuary is a vital cultural and ecological site, safeguarding both marine life and the remains of the Great Lakes' shipping history. Anchored by the Great Lakes Maritime Heritage Center in Alpena, it offers visitors a unique glimpse into underwater archaeology, diving adventures, and the area's rich cultural past.

7 Wisconsin Shipwreck Coast National Marine Sanctuary

The Wisconsin Shipwreck Coast National Marine Sanctuary, designated in 2021, spans 726 square nautical miles (962 square miles) along Lake Michigan's coast in Wisconsin. Comanaged by NOAA and the State of Wisconsin, it protects 36 known shipwrecks from the 19th and early 20th centuries, including some remarkably well preserved due to the cold freshwater. These shipwrecks, now archaeological treasures, reflect the region's maritime heritage, connecting Wisconsin to other Great Lakes ports. The sanctuary stretches across 82 miles of coastline and four counties and is vital in preserving cultural heritage while offering insights into marine history and ecosystem conservation.

8 Lake Ontario National Marine Sanctuary

Designated in 2024, Lake Ontario National Marine Sanctuary is the most recent and 16th addition to the United States National Marine Sanctuary System. Covering an expansive area of 1,722 square miles in eastern Lake Ontario, this sanctuary is a significant cultural and ecological treasure. It preserves a diverse array of marine life, including rich underwater forests, plants, and aquatic animals, while protecting an invaluable cultural heritage. The sanctuary is home to some of the best preserved shipwrecks and archaeological sites in the world, reflecting centuries of maritime history, from the early indigenous inhabitants, such as the Haudenosaunee Confederacy, to the bustling commerce and trade that shaped the region. Comanaged by NOAA and New York State, the sanctuary offers opportunities for research, education, and community engagement, fostering a deep connection to the past and a commitment to preserving this unique environment for future generations.

9 Stellwagen Bank National Marine Sanctuary

The Stellwagen Bank National Marine Sanctuary, covering 842 square miles at the entrance of Massachusetts Bay between Cape Cod and Cape Ann, is a protected marine area celebrated for its rich biodiversity and historical significance. Established in 1992, this sanctuary plays a vital role in preserving a diverse array of marine life, including over 130 species such as humpback whales, Atlantic cod, and leatherback sea turtles. Notably, it is a premier whale watching destination where visitors can observe several whale species, including the endangered North Atlantic right whale. The sanctuary also safeguards the area's rich cultural heritage, which dates back to its discovery by early explorers and its significance as a fishing ground since the 17th century. Its unique underwater plateau, Stellwagen Bank, fosters nutrient rich upwellings that support this vibrant ecosystem.

10   Mallows Bay Potomac River National Marine Sanctuary

Mallows BayPotomac River National Marine Sanctuary, located in Charles County, Maryland, spans 18 square miles along the Potomac River. Designated on September 9, 2019, this sanctuary is renowned for preserving the "Ghost Fleet," the largest collection of shipwrecks in the Western Hemisphere, with over 230 sunken vessels, including World War Iera wooden steamships. These shipwrecks have transformed into artificial reefs, fostering a rich habitat that supports diverse marine life, plants, and wildlife. Beyond its ecological significance, Mallows Bay also protects a wealth of cultural heritage, offering a unique glimpse into early 20th century maritime history.

11   Monitor National Marine Sanctuary

The Monitor National Marine Sanctuary, located 16 nautical miles southsoutheast of Cape Hatteras, North Carolina, encompasses a 1nautical mile wide column of water that stretches from the ocean's surface to the seabed, covering an area centered around the wreck of the USS Monitor. This sanctuary, established on January 30, 1975, as the first national marine sanctuary in the United States, preserves the remains of the Civil War ironclad warship, which revolutionized naval warfare. Covering approximately 1 square nautical mile, the sanctuary protects not only this historic cultural resource but also acts as an artificial reef that supports diverse marine life, including species like amberjack and black sea bass. The site is a significant cultural and ecological treasure, with artifacts from the Monitor now preserved and displayed in various museums.

12   Gray's Reef National Marine Sanctuary

Gray's Reef National Marine Sanctuary, located 19 miles off Sapelo Island, Georgia, is one of the largest nearshore live bottom reefs in the southeastern United States. Covering an area of 22 square miles, this sanctuary was designated in January 1981 and is a vital part of the U.S National Marine Sanctuary System. The reef features rocky sandstone outcrop and sandy flats submerged under 60 to 70 feet of water, creating a complex habitat that supports diverse marine life, including fish and invertebrates Beyond its ecological significance, Gray's Reef also preserves cultural heritage as it was once dry land over 8,000 years ago, with evidence of human occupation dating back more than 13,250 years.

13 Flower Garden Banks National Marine Sanctuary

The Flower Garden Banks Sanctuary is a significant marine protected area located approximately 100 nautical miles (190 km) off the coast of Galveston, Texas, in the northwestern Gulf of Mexico. Established in 1992 and expanded in 2021, the sanctuary now covers 160 square miles (415 square kilometers). It preserves the northernmost coral reefs in the United States, which thrive on seamounts formed by underlying salt domes. FGBNMS is home to nearly 300 species of fish, over 20 coral species, and various marine mammals, sharks, rays, and sea turtles. The sanctuary also protects cultural heritage sites and provides critical habitat for endangered species.

14 Florida Keys National Marine Sanctuary

Set up in 1990, the Florida Keys National Marine Sanctuary extends over 3,800 square miles of waters surrounding the Keys. It is home to North America's only coral barrier reef, extensive seagrass beds, and thousands of species of marine life. Additionally, the sanctuary safeguards cultural heritage sites, such as shipwrecks, that reflect the region's rich maritime history.

15 Hawaiian Islands Humpback Whale National Marine Sanctuary

The Hawaiian Islands Humpback Whale Sanctuary, set up by the U.S. Congress in 1992, covers 1,400 square miles (3,600 km²) of ocean surrounding the Hawaiian Islands. This sanctuary is one of the world's most crucial habitats for the endangered North Pacific humpback whale, hosting thousands each winter as they migrate to breed, nurse, and mate. The sanctuary protects a rich diversity of marine life, including endemic coral reefs and seagrass beds. It also preserves the cultural heritage of Native Hawaiians, who have a deep, historical connection to these waters. Through research, education, and public engagement, the sanctuary promotes the long term conservation of these majestic creatures and their habitat, balancing ecological protection with sustainable human activities.

16 National Marine Sanctuary of American Samoa

Founded in 1986, the National Marine Sanctuary of American Samoa is a pristine underwater treasure spanning an impressive 13,581 square miles in the South Pacific. This federally protected area, the largest and most remote in the United States, boasts exceptional marine biodiversity, including ancient coral reefs, hydrothermal vents, and rare archaeological sites. Home to a myriad of marine life, from vibrant coral species to majestic humpback whales, the sanctuary plays a crucial role in preserving delicate ecosystems. Its significance extends beyond ecology, encompassing a rich cultural heritage deeply intertwined with the Samoan people. While facing threats like climate change and human impact, ongoing research and conservation efforts strive to safeguard this natural wonder for generations to come.

INTERNATIONAL Additional Sanctuaries

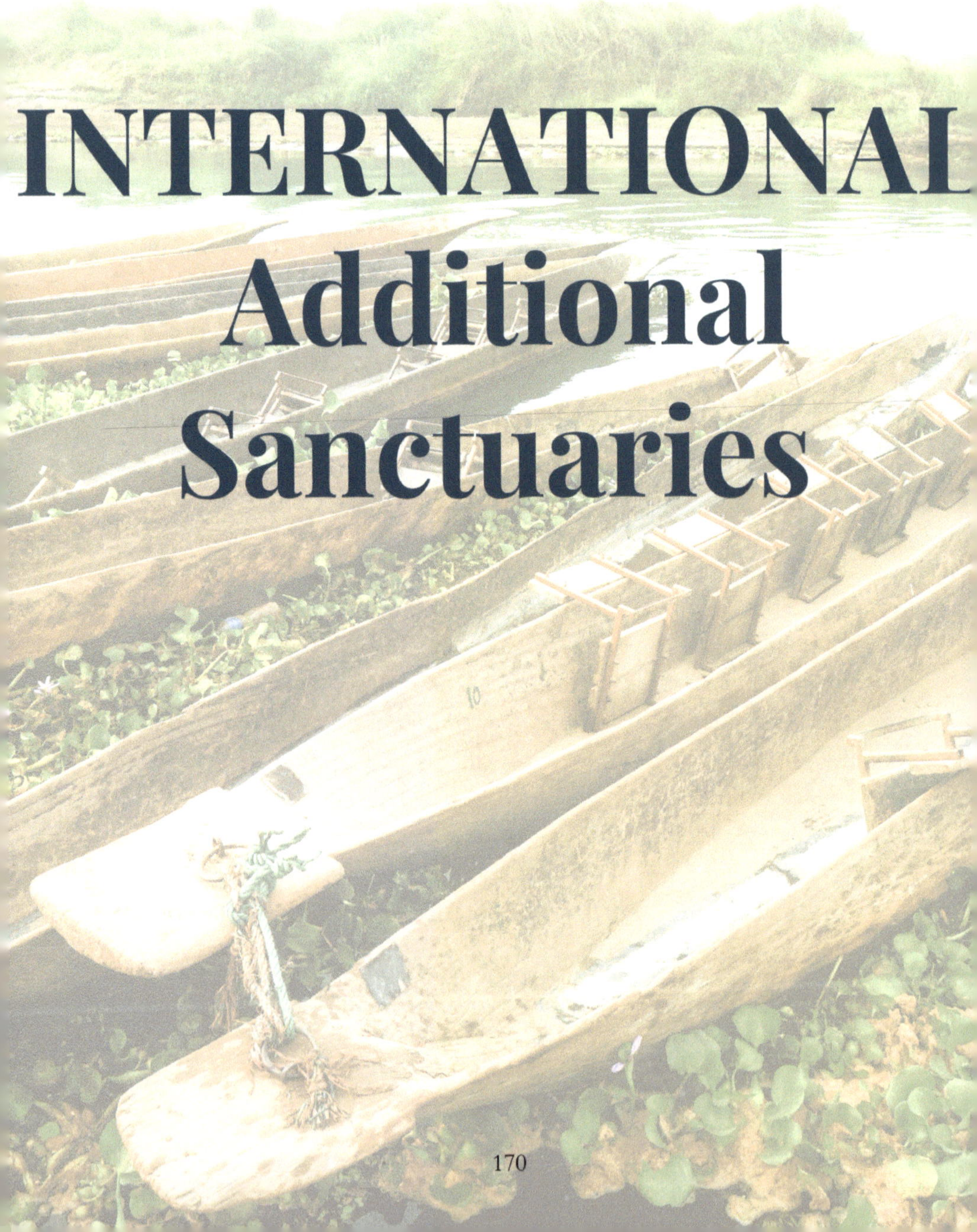

Africa

Africa's marine sanctuaries are as diverse as the continent itself, boasting some of the most remarkable ecosystems on Earth, such as Goukamma Marine Protected Area in South Africa, Nosy Be and Surrounding Marine Reserves in Madagascar, Bazaruto Archipelago National Park in Mozambique, Quirimbas Archipelago in Mozambique, Ras Mohammed National Park in Egypt, Watamu Marine National Park in Kenya, Cape Verde Archipelago in Cape Verde, Mafia Island Marine Park in Tanzania, and iSimangaliso Wetland Park in South Africa. Among these, the Bazaruto Archipelago in Mozambique stands out as a critical marine protected area. Located off the coast of Vilankulo, this group of six islands is home to the largest population of dugongs on the African continent. The archipelago's waters are also rich in coral reefs, seagrass beds, and mangrove forests, creating a haven for species like humpback whales, dolphins, and various shark species. Established as a national park in 1971, the Bazaruto Archipelago National Park covers over 1,400 square kilometers of protected marine and terrestrial habitats. This sanctuary is not only crucial for biodiversity conservation but also for the livelihood of local communities that depend on sustainable fishing and ecotourism.

Another significant sanctuary in Africa is the Aldabra Atoll, part of the Seychelles, one of the most remote and least disturbed coral atolls in the world. Aldabra is a UNESCO World Heritage Site known for its rich marine life, including the largest population of giant tortoises and important nesting grounds for green turtles. It was officially recognized a UNESCO World Heritage Site in 1982 and extends over 60 sq miles. The Atoll's marine environment is equally impressive, with a vibrant underwater landscape of coral reefs and deep channels that support a diverse array of species, including manta rays and reef sharks. Aldabra's isolation has allowed it to remain relatively unspoiled by human activity, providing a critical refuge for species that are vulnerable elsewhere.

Conservation efforts in Aldabra are led by the Seychelles Islands Foundation which works to preserve this pristine environment against the threats of climate change and illegal fishing.

The Middle East

The Middle East is home to several significant marine sanctuaries, but the UAE stands out with its extensive efforts in marine conservation. The country has established 16 marine protected areas, covering over 12% of its marine territory. These areas are critical in protecting habitats like coral reefs, mangroves, and seagrass beds, which are vital for species such as green and hawksbill turtles. The Marwah and Al Yasat Reserves in Abu Dhabi, established in 2007 and 2005 respectively, among others, contribute to preserving the region's biodiversity, providing sanctuary for various marine species, and ensuring the sustainability of fish stocks through stringent protection measures.

Further strengthening these efforts is the UAE's commitment to the Global Ocean Alliance, a coalition of 32 countries dedicated to safeguarding at least 30% of the world's oceans by 2030. The UAE's flagship marine research vessel 'Jaywun,' is central to these conservation initiatives. Equipped with stateoftheart research facilities, 'Jaywun' conducts comprehensive surveys of the marine environment, assessing the impacts of climate change and monitoring biodiversity. This vessel not only aids in scientific research but also supports the development of strategies for the sustainable management of marine resources, ensuring that the UAE remains a leader in marine conservation in the region.

Russia

Russia's vast coastline, stretching across the Arctic and Pacific Oceans, is home to some of the world's most diverse and ecologically significant marine sanctuaries. Among these, the Commander Islands Biosphere Reserve in the

Bering Sea, founded in 1993, stands out as a crucial habitat for numerous marine species, including sea otters, fur seals, and over a million seabirds. This remote archipelago, part of the Russian Far East, plays a vital role in preserving the biodiversity of the North Pacific, providing a refuge for endangered species and a critical area for scientific research on marine ecosystems. Similarly, the Wrangel Island Reserve, which was established in 1976, located in the Arctic Ocean, is recognized as a UNESCO World Heritage Site and serves as a key breeding ground for polar bears, walruses, and migratory birds, making it a cornerstone of Russia's Arctic conservation efforts.

In addition to these highprofile reserves, Russia has established several other marine protected areas across its vast territories, each contributing to the preservation of its unique marine environments. The Far Eastern State Marine Biosphere Reserve, located in the Sea of Japan and founded in 1978, protects a rich diversity of marine life, including rare species of fish and invertebrates, as well as important kelp forests and coral reefs. Meanwhile, the Great Arctic State Nature Reserve, founded in 1993, the largest in Russia and one of the largest globally, safeguards the fragile ecosystems of the Arctic tundra and coastal areas, which are increasingly threatened by climate change. These sanctuaries not only support the conservation of critical habitats but also play a significant role in Russia's broader environmental protection strategies, balancing ecological preservation with sustainable resource use.

Australia

Australia's marine conservation efforts are among the most extensive globally, with 60 Australian Marine Parks managed by the government covering 3.8 million square kilometers of Commonwealth waters. These parks, located more than 5.5 kilometers from the coast, play a crucial role in preserving marine habitats and species. Management plans guide the protection and sustainable use of these parks, with distinct plans for each of the five marine park networks and the Coral Sea.

In addition to these parks, Australia's National Representative System of Marine Protected Areas includes the iconic Great Barrier Reef Marine Park which was founded in 1975 and is overseen by the Great Barrier Reef Authority, and the Heard Island and McDonald Islands Marine Reserve, which was founded in 2002, is overseen by the Australian Antarctic Division. Together, these protected areas cover nearly half of Australia's waters, making it one of the largest and most comprehensive marine protection networks in the world.

India

India's coastline, spanning over 7,500 kilometers, is home to a rich diversity of marine life, yet our understanding of this underwater world remains limited. To protect and explore this biodiversity, India has established several marine national parks and sanctuaries. Founded in 1980, the Gulf of Kutch in Gujarat, India's first Marine National Park, offers a unique glimpse into marine ecosystems with its 52 species of corals and various marine mammals. Similarly, the Mahatma Gandhi Marine National Park in the Andaman (1983) and Nicobar Islands serves as a haven for endangered coral reefs and sea turtles and is known for its scuba diving opportunities.

Other significant marine sanctuaries include the Gulf of Mannar Marine National Park in Tamil Nadu (1986), known for its endangered dugongs and diverse marine flora, and the Gahirmatha Marine Sanctuary in Odisha (1977), famed for hosting millions of Olive Ridley turtles during their nesting season. The Malvan Marine Wildlife Sanctuary in Maharashtra (1987), though smaller in size, is celebrated for its rich biodiversity and opportunities for water sports. These sanctuaries play a great role in conserving India's marine heritage, offering a blend of ecological richness and recreational activities.

Pakistan

Pakistan's marine ecosystems are safeguarded by a network of Marine Protected Areas (MPAs) that play a crucial role in preserving the country's coastal and marine biodiversity. These include Keti Bunder South, Marho Kotri, Hingol National Park, and Astola Island Marine Protected Area, collectively covering over 1,161 square kilometers. Astola Island, in particular, stands out as Pakistan's first Marine Protected Area, which was designated in 2017. Located in the Arabian Sea, Astola Island is a biodiversity haven, home to several endangered species, comprising the green turtle and the hawksbill turtle. The island's coral reefs, seagrass beds, and sandy beaches provide vital habitats for these species while also supporting a variety of marine life, such as dolphins, fish, and seabirds.

The MPAs in Pakistan are significant not only for their environmental importance but also for their cultural and economic roles. These areas are integral to the livelihoods of local fishing communities, which depend on the sustainable management of marine resources. In Hingol National Park, the largest of Pakistan's MPAs, efforts are being made to balance conservation with the needs of these communities. The park's diverse ecosystems, ranging from coastal mangroves to desert landscapes, support a wide array of wildlife, including the endangered Arabian humpback whale and various species of migratory birds. However, these fragile ecosystems face threats from overfishing, pollution, and climate change, making ongoing conservation efforts vital for preserving Pakistan's marine heritage for future generations.

Western Europe

Western Europe is host to some of the world's most wellpreserved marine sanctuaries, with a strong focus on balancing conservation and sustainable use. The NorthEast Atlantic and the Mediterranean Sea host a range of Marine Protected Areas (MPAs) that protect diverse ecosystems, from the cold waters of the Arctic Circle to the warm, temperate zones of southern Europe. Notable examples include the OSPAR Convention's network of MPAs, which covers over 5 million square kilometers and is dedicated to preserving the biodiversity of the NorthEast Atlantic. It officially started operating in 1972. These areas protect critical habitats, such as deepsea coral reefs, seagrass meadows, and migratory routes for marine mammals, also including the critically endangered North Atlantic right whale.

In addition to their environmental significance, Western Europe's MPAs play a crucial role in supporting local economies through sustainable fisheries and ecotourism. For instance, the Wadden Sea, shared by Denmark, Germany, and the Netherlands, is not only a UNESCO World Heritage Site but also one of the most productive ecosystems in the world. It harbors a rich diversity of marine life and acts as an important breeding ground for numerous bird species. Conservation efforts across Western Europe are increasingly focused on addressing challenges such as overfishing, marine pollution, and the impacts of climate change, ensuring that these protected areas continue to thrive for generations to come.

Japan

Japan, an island nation surroundedby diverse marine ecosystems, is home to several important marine sanctuaries that reflect its commitment to the conservation and sustainable use of ocean resources. The Ogasawara Islands, a UNESCOrecognized World Heritage Site, are one of Japan's most significant marine protected areas, known for their unique biodiversity, including endemic species of fish, coral, and invertebrates. These remote islands were founded in 1972 and are located about 1,000 kilometers south of Tokyo. They feature pristine coral reefs, deepsea hydrothermal vents, and rich marine habitats that provide refuge for species like humpback whales and green turtles. The government has implemented stringent conservation measures to protect this delicate environment from threats like illegal fishing and invasive species, ensuring that the Ogasawara Islands remain a sanctuary for future generations.

Another key marine sanctuary in Japan is the Shiretoko Peninsula, located in the northernmost part of Hokkaido. Shiretoko, also recognized as a UNESCO World Heritage Site in 2005, boasts a diverse range of ecosystems that include coastal waters rich in marine life, such as sea lions, salmon, and orcas. The area's cold currents create nutrientrich waters that support high biodiversity, making it a crucial breeding and feeding ground for many marine species. Conservation efforts in Shiretoko focus on maintaining the balance between human activities, like sustainable fisheries and ecotourism, and the preservation of nature. The blending of traditional knowledge with modern conservation practices has allowed Japan to protect these marine sanctuaries while supporting local communities.

China

China's vast coastline and its proximity to crucial marine ecosystems have led to the establishment of several key marine sanctuaries aimed at protecting biodiversity and promoting sustainable development. The South China Sea is home to one of the country's largest marine protected areas, the Sanya Coral Reef National Nature Reserve. Located in Hainan Province and designated in 1990, this reserve protects over 85 square kilometers of coral reefs, mangroves and seagrass beds, supporting a wide array of marine life, including rare and endangered species like the dugong and the hawksbill turtle. Efforts to restore and maintain these ecosystems have involved coral reef restoration projects, strict fishing regulations, and public education campaigns, highlighting China's growing emphasis on marine conservation in the face of rapid coastal development and industrialization.

In addition to its southern waters, China's northern coastline is protected b the Yellow Sea Wetland Reserve, a critical habitat for migratory birds an marine species. Spanning over 2,000 square kilometers, this reserve is part c the East AsianAustralasian Flyway, one of the world's most importar migratory bird routes. The wetland is crucial for species like the spoonbille sandpiper and the Chinese egret, both of which rely on this area during the migratory journeys. Beyond avian conservation, the reserve's coastal waters ar home to significant fishery resources and vital nursery grounds for marin species, making it essential for both biodiversity and local livelihoods.

DIRECTORY OF OCEANIC LIFE

List of Ocean Related Animals and Species, Organized Alphabetically, with 5 to 7 Sea Life ExamplesforEachLetter:

A

1. Angelfish
2. Anemone
3. Atlantic Cod
4. Arctic Char
5. Arowana
6. Abalone
7. Australian Ghost Shark

B

1. Blue Whale
2. Barracuda
3. Atlantic Cod
4. Beluga Whale
5. Barnacle
6. Bottlenose Dolphin
7. Basking Shark

C

1. Clownfish
2. Crab
3. Coral
4. Catshark
5. Cuttlefish
6. Coelacanth
7. Cod

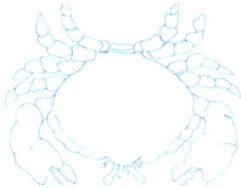

D

1. Dolphin
2. Dugong
3. Dory (Royal Blue Tang)
4. Devil Ray
5. Dungeness Crab
6. Dogfish
7. Dumbo Octopus

E

1. Eel
2. Elephant Seal
3. Emperor Shrimp
4. Epaulette Shark
5. European Sea Bass
6. Encrusting Sponge
7. Elkhorn Coral

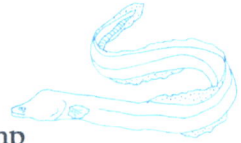

F

1. Flying Fish
2. Flounder
3. Fire Coral
4. Fangtooth Fish
5. Fiddler Crab
6. Feather Star
7. Fin Whale

G

1. Giant Squid
2. Great White Shark
3. Grouper
4. Giant Clam
5. Green Sea Turtle
6. Galapagos Shark
7. Goosefish

H

1. Humpback Whale
2. Hammerhead Shark
3. Hagfish
4. Harlequin Shrimp
5. Horseshoe Crab
6. Haddock 7. Herring

I

1. Isopod
2. Iridescent Shark
3. Indian Mackerel
4. Ivory Coral
5. Iberian Rock Lizardfish
6. Indigo Hamlet
7. Icefish

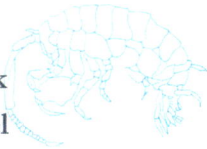

J

1. Jellyfish
2. Japanese Spider Crab
3. Jawfish
4. Jewel Anemone
5. Jack Mackerel
6. Javanese Cownose Ray
7. Japanese Sea Nettle

K

1. Killer Whale (Orca)
2. King Crab
3. Krill
4. Kelp Bass
5. Kitefin Shark
6. Kuhlia (Flagtail)
7. King Mackerel

L

1. Lobster
2. Leafy Seadragon
3. Lionfish
4. Leatherback Turtle
5. Lumpfish
6. Longfin Squid
7. Lamprey

M

1. Manatee
2. Manta Ray
3. Marlin
4. Moray Eel
5. Moon Jellyfish
6. Megamouth Shark
7. Mantis Shrimp

N

1. Nudibranch
2. Nurse Shark
3. Napoleon Wrasse
4. Northern Pufferfish
5. Needlefish
6. Nautilus
7. Neritic Squid

O

1. Octopus
2. Orca
3. Oarfish
4. Olive Ridley Sea Turtle
5. Ocean Sunfish (Mola Mola)
6. Oyster
7. Opah

S

1. Starfish
2. Seahorse
3. Swordfish
4. Squid

P

1. Parrotfish
2. Pufferfish
3. Porpoise
4. Penguin
5. Pilot Whale
6. Peacock Mantis Shrimp
7. Pipefish

Q

1. Queen Conch
2. Queen Triggerfish
3. Quahog Clam
4. Quillback Rockfish
5. Queensland Grouper
6. QuasiAncistrus Catfish

R

1. Red Snapper
2. Ray
3. Rockfish
4. Ribbon Eel
5. Risso's Dolphin
6. Remora
7. Reef Shark

5. Sea Lion
6. Sea Urchin
7. Salmon

T

1. Tiger Shark
2. Tuna
3. Thresher Shark
4. Triggerfish
5. Toadfish
6. Tuskfish
7. Turbot

U

1. Urchin
2. Umbrella Squid
3. UpsideDown Jellyfish
4. Uaru Fish
5. Ulysses Wrasse
6. Undulate Ray
7. Uchiwa Shrimp

V

1. Vaquita
2. Velvet Crab
3. Viperfish
4. Venus Clam
5. Vermilion Snapper
6. Velella (Bythewind Sailor)
7. Volcano Barnacle

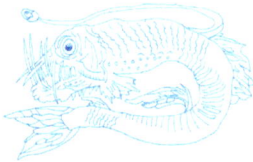

W

1. Walrus
2. Whale Shark
3. Wobbegong Shark
4. Wrasse
5. Whiting
6. Warty Sea Cucumber
7. White Marlin

X

1. Xiphias (Swordfish)
2. Xantho Crab
3. Xanthichthys (Triggerfish)
4. Xingu Corydoras
5. Xiphosura (Horseshoe Crab)

Y

1. Yellowfin Tuna
2. Yellowtail Snapper
3. Yellow Tang
4. Yeti Crab
5. Yellow Seahorse
6. Yarrell's Blenny
7. Yakka (Yellowtail Scad)

Z

1. Zebra Shark
2. Zooplankton
3. Zebra Moray
4. Zebra Mussel
5. Zebrafish
6. Zebra Sea Urchin

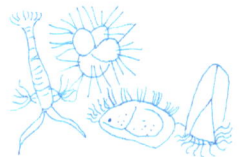